C000117924

Double Headers

Keith Walmsley

First published in Great Britain by
Association of Cricket Statisticians and Historians
Cardiff CF11 9XR.
© ACS, 2013
Keith Walmsley has asserted his right under the Copyright, Designs
and Patents Act 1988 to be identified as the author of this work

All Rights Reserved. No part of this publication may be reproduced, stored in a
retrieval system, or transmitted in any form, or by any means, electronic,
mechanical, photocopying, recording or otherwise without the prior permission in
writing of the Copyright holders, nor be otherwise circulated in any form, or
binding or cover other than in which it is published and without a similar condition
including this condition being imposed on the subsequent publisher.

British Library Cataloguing-in-Publication Data.
A catalogue record for this book is available from the British Library.

ISBN: 978-1-908165-37-4
Typeset and printed by The City Press Leeds Ltd

Contents

Introduction

Many books have been written about, or around, individual cricket matches. Generally, what made those matches special were events that took place during the game itself – perhaps an outstanding batting or bowling performance, or an exceptional recovery by a team that looked well beaten, or whatever.

This book also started life looking at a single cricket match - Surrey's game against Oxford University at Reigate in June 1909. But in this instance what made the match of special interest wasn't something that happened on the field of play. What made the match remarkable was the fact that it took place at all, and that right from the start it was accepted without any challenge into the canon of first-class matches.

For at the same time as Surrey were playing at Reigate, another Surrey side was playing a County Championship match against Lancashire 20 miles away at The Oval. Originally, I had thought simply to explore the whys and wherefores of what, at first sight, was surely a unique instance of an English side playing two simultaneous first-class matches.

But the unusual nature of this occurrence led me to start looking for other instances, both in England and elsewhere. It turns out that there are over two dozen instances in England alone, and many more overseas.

But in only one other instance in England was it a county side that doubled up. This was in 1919, when Warwickshire played a championship match at Derby early in August, on the same dates as another Warwickshire side was playing a non-championship match against Worcestershire at Edgbaston. Unlike the Surrey instance – where there has never been any doubt about the first-class status of both the matches concerned – the status of the game at Edgbaston in 1919 is still disputed in some quarters over 90 years later. After due consideration, the ACS accepted it as first-class several years ago, and I am content to accept the Association's view on this matter.

So the original aim of this book itself quickly doubled up. The first two chapters now concentrate on these two main 'double-headers' in England, seeking to bring together, as far as can now be traced, the why, where, who and what of these two instances, with particular reference to the 'lesser' (non-Championship) match in each case.

However, the completist in me would not be satisfied if I didn't also identify and comment on other instances of doubling-up – or in some cases 'tripling-up' - both in England and around the world. So I have sought to cover this area in Chapters 3 to 10.

I have used the term 'double-header' to refer to such occurrences as a term of convenience, although I acknowledge that it doesn't exactly match any of the established definitions of the term, sporting or non-sporting. In this book I have used the term to refer to any instance when two first-class matches were in play, or were scheduled to be in play, on the same day or days that involved either

· two sides representing the same cricketing entity , or

· two sides representing the same geographical or administrative entity, or

· two sides in the same country bearing the same name.

Some near misses, when that definition was nearly but not quite fully satisfied, are also noted.

I don't pretend that the events and occurrences that this book describes are of any particular moment in the wider scheme of things, but I hope that they might intrigue a certain type of cricket-follower. Or as Abraham Lincoln (and later Jean Brodie) put it, that "people who like this sort of thing will find this the sort of thing they like". That will do for me.

1: Surrey in 1909

Surrey v Lancashire (The Oval) and
Surrey v Oxford University (Reigate), June 1909

HOW DID IT COME ABOUT?

Misapprehensions

My first encounter with Surrey's 1909 double-header came as a result of an e-mail in 2005 from George A.Smith of Hove, who queried:

"Is there any other occasion when because of a fixtures mix-up a first-class team fielded two sides simultaneously?"

Mr Smith is not alone in assuming that the doubling-up occurred because of some sort of backstage cock-up. Jack Hobbs – who played in one of the 1909 matches – and his biographer John Arlott seem to have been under the same apprehension:

"[1909] was an odd season for Surrey. Owing to an administrative muddle which delighted Jack Hobbs's dry sense of humour, they were scheduled to play two first-class home fixtures – against Lancashire and the return with Oxford University – on the same three days."

John Arlott: Jack Hobbs – Profile of the Master (John Murray, 1981).

Others have fought shy of suggesting or investigating a reason for the double-header:

"For reasons it is now difficult to comprehend, Surrey had arranged to meet Oxford University at Reigate on the same days that they were entertaining Lancashire at The Oval and therefore engaged in two first-class matches at one and the same time."

David Lemmon: The History of Surrey CCC (Helm, 1989)

Whereas yet others are more confident of the reason:

"A rather unfortunate error in the arrangement of fixtures for this season gave Surrey a match with Oxford University at Reigate when, in fact, the County had a match with Lancashire."

Gordon Ross: The Surrey Story (Stanley Paul, 1957)

But all these writers were wrong. Surrey's 1909 double-header was no fixtures mix-up, no administrative muddle; and it certainly was not an 'unfortunate error'. The following pages give the true explanation, as far as it can be deduced from surviving sources.[1]

Fixture pressures

When the County Championship was formalised in 1890, most of the first-class counties sought to play all their rivals home and away each season. But for most, this was impossible, or impractical, after the expansion of the Championship in 1895, and only three counties sought to maintain the practice after that date.

---

[1] The sources used for the background to the 1909 double-header consist principally of Surrey CCC Committee Minutes now held at the Surrey History Centre at Woking, especially those under references 2042/1/6, 2042/1/7, 2042/3/2 and 3035/8/6. Unfortunately no records survive from either Oxford University CC or Reigate Priory CC which might shed further light on the origin of the double-header fixtures.

Yorkshire managed to arrange a 'full set' of Championship fixtures in every season up to and including 1901, and did so again in 1904. Lancashire also did so in most (though not all) seasons up to 1901, but in these early days Surrey were the most persistent 'full-setters', arranging to play all their opponents twice in every season from 1890 to 1908 apart from 1899 (when they missed out on fixtures against newly-first-class Worcestershire), and the years from 1905 to 1907 when they declined to play Somerset, with whom they were in dispute.[2] When that dispute was settled, in 1908 Surrey again arranged a full set of fixtures, becoming the first side ever to schedule as many as 30 Championship matches in a single season.

Meanwhile, with ever more frequent tours by overseas teams, and with a gradual rise in the number of fixtures between the counties and the Universities, the first-class fixture list was steadily expanding, rising from 79 in 1890 to 214 in 1908.

Surrey were one of the busier counties over this period. As well as looking to play 30 Championship matches each year by 1908, they also looked to play two matches each year against the principal touring side, and also to play both Universities at least once, and preferably twice (home and away), in each season.[3] Adding in their early-season matches against London County, or against an equivalent side styled 'W.G.Grace's XI' or 'Gentlemen of England', their total number of first-class fixtures each season between 1900 and 1908 was between 33 and 36.

Overall, between 1890 and 1908, Surrey arranged 551 first-class matches, a figure exceeded only by Yorkshire with 565. No other county had arranged more than Lancashire's 487. And whereas some counties used several grounds for their home fixtures - Yorkshire, for example, usually used seven or eight home grounds in each season - Surrey used only a single ground for all their home matches.

The Oval was Surrey's only home ground: no home county matches had been played anywhere else since 1854. Its location and standing meant that it was also in demand for other high-profile fixtures – a Test match in every Australian season and in the South African season of 1907, an annual Gentlemen v Players match in mid-July, the annual Champion County v The Rest fixture from 1903, and occasional other first-class matches such as Surrey v England in 1895, and non-Surrey fixtures involving the Philadelphians in both 1897 and 1903.

Until 1905, The Oval was also the only home venue used by Surrey's Second XI, and was also used for between six and ten Club & Ground fixtures each season. Surrey CCC also made it available for an occasional 'day let' to worthy clubs and organisations from within the local community or wider afield in Surrey.

In summary, by 1909 The Oval was hugely in demand by a county club

---

2   The dispute related to what in modern football parlance would be referred to as an alleged 'illegal approach' by Somerset to the Surrey player Bill Montgomery.

3   Between 1890 and 1908, Surrey played 45 first-class matches against the Universities - almost twice as many as any other county apart from Sussex (39).

that sought wherever possible to play all its county rivals both home and away each season, to play both Universities at home each season, to play one or two tourist matches each season, and to play at least some Second XI and Club & Ground fixtures on the ground as well as allowing some community use of it; and also by the wider cricketing authorities for the accommodation of around three or four 'prestige' matches each year, including a Test match in an increasing proportion of seasons.

Surrey's fixture list for 1909

As far as the county club was concerned, at the outset the 1909 season looked no different from earlier years. Fixture planning for the season had begun as early as July 1908, when Surrey's Match Committee recommended that, although the match against W.G.Grace's side should now be dropped (no doubt not unconnected to the fact that W.G. himself had now finally retired), both Oxford and Cambridge Universities should be met at The Oval.[4]

Next month the club's full Committee decided to refer back to the Match Committee "the question of playing Out and Home matches with the Universities of Oxford and Cambridge".[5] So whereas in 1908 Surrey had played only two matches against the Universities, the full Committee seemed to have been encouraging the idea of playing four such matches in 1909, despite the inevitable pressure for other fixtures at The Oval during an Australian summer.

The matter bounced back and forth between the Match Committee and the full Committee over the next couple of months, and no final decision had yet been taken when, on 15 October, the full Committee resolved "that out and home matches should, *if possible* [my emphasis], be played against the Universities of Oxford and Cambridge".

But crucially to one of the themes of this book, that minute is preceded by this:
Surrey v Oxford University
"It was decided to play a Surrey XI against Oxford University in 1909 in Surrey, but not at the Oval, owing to the Oval not being available on the dates Oxford can offer."

So here is the first piece in the jigsaw that led to the double-header of June 1909: a decision to play a home fixture against Oxford University away from The Oval.

Frustratingly, there is nothing in the minutes either at this time, or over the next few months, about the timetabling or choice of venue of the University match. There is nothing in the surviving minutes that even acknowledges the fact that the match would be played on the same dates as a County Championship match, let alone anything the considers the wisdom or propriety of playing two first-class matches simultaneously.

All we know is that the decisions about date and venue were made somewhere between 15 October and 8 December 1908. On the latter

4   Minutes of the Surrey CCC Match Committee meeting of 27 July 1908.
5   Minutes of the Surrey CCC Committee meeting of 6 August 1908.

date, the full fixture list for 1909 was confirmed at the annual meeting of County Secretaries, the outcome of which was reported to Surrey's Committee on 17 December. By Christmas the fixture list was in the public domain: the issue of *Cricket* dated 24 December published the programme for the season, including on 21 June three-day games between Surrey and Lancashire at The Oval, and between Surrey and Oxford University at Reigate. This same fixture list was given a degree of finality with its inclusion on page 530 of *Wisden* for 1909, published at the end of January 1909.

Fixture congestion: the evidence

Was it really impractical to find a slot at The Oval for the Oxford University fixture? Assuming that primacy had to be given to County Championship and tourist matches, the answer must be 'Yes'. Between 3 May and the end of the University season on 7 July, Surrey were scheduled to play 17 Championship matches (eight at The Oval and nine away), and a three-day fixture against the Australians. The only three-day period when Surrey were not playing a county match between early May and early July was 13-15 May. Apart from this, and the break for the Gentlemen v Players matches in mid-July, the Surrey First XI had not a single break between the start of their season on 3 May and its end on 1 September.

The 13-15 May slot was filled by the match against Oxford University in The Parks. It fell at the beginning of the University's first-class season, and in view of Surrey's enthusiasm to play the universities twice each, it was an easy choice to insert this match into the programme. Using this slot for Surrey's home fixture against Oxford would have solved nothing - it would simply have shifted the problem to finding a slot for Surrey's desired away fixture with Oxford; and besides, it would have been entirely against precedent for Oxford to have played a first-class match away from Oxford so early in the season .

Meanwhile, the programme for The Oval was pretty much full to bursting too. When the First XI was playing elsewhere, The Oval was required for four two-day Second XI matches and five days of Club and Ground games. When the county's full Committee met in October 1908, it had duly noted that The Oval was "not ... available on the dates Oxford can offer".

With a decision that The Oval was not available for a game against Oxford, a further matter fell for consideration. Was there scope for Oxford to fit in an away game against Surrey somewhere other than The Oval, without interfering with the Championship programme?

The short answer is no. With the match against Surrey at Oxford now in place on 13-14-15 May, the University's first-class season ran from 13 May to 7 July, with a series of home fixtures up to 19 June being followed (after a break between 20 and 23 June) by a block of away matches, leading up to the University Match on 5 July. As already explained, Surrey were solidly booked for the whole of this period, for County Championship matches and a game against the Australians.

The fact is that there was simply no room in the two sides' crowded fixture lists to fit in a three-day game that did not clash with some other fixture. Even if Oxford had been prepared to break with tradition and play this away game during (or even before) their normal home season, or to play it after the University Match, there were no realistic slots available in Surrey's and The Oval's programmes. The only such slot theoretically available was 12-14 July, during the Lord's Gentlemen v Players Match. But not only would this be unlikely to have been much of an attraction to the paying public, given the much more attractive (on paper at least) fixture on the other side of the Thames, it would also have been a full week after an already-late University Match, and as such unlikely to have been a great attraction to the leading University players.

So the unavoidable conclusion was reached that the only way for a fixture to be arranged in Surrey between the county and Oxford University in 1909 was for it to be doubled up with an existing fixture. Quite why the county club chose to follow this option is unclear. Their pre-season aim had been to play home and away fixtures with both Oxford and Cambridge "if possible". In the event they played Oxford twice but Cambridge not at all. In view of the difficulties in arranging the second Oxford fixture, it is very surprising that the county club decided to pursue it – after all, if they were prepared to give up the matches against Cambridge in this crowded season, was the second Oxford fixture really so essential?

Unfortunately there is nothing in the surviving records that even addresses this question, let alone answers it. So we can only speculate.

Did the fact that Surrey's captain, H.D.G. 'Shrimp' Leveson Gower, was an old Oxford man have any influence in deciding that the second Oxford fixture was "possible" despite the apparent practical difficulties in fixing it? Or was it just that those deciding on Surrey's fixtures were unwilling to arrange only a single match against the Universities, regardless of the implications – after all, Surrey had played at least two matches against Oxford and/or Cambridge in each year since 1898? Or was it perhaps that the second fixture was agreed as something of a trial effort, to see if there was support for taking the occasional county match away from The Oval?

On this last point, some contemporary reports of the games in 1909 refer to the double-header as "an experiment", as if Surrey were trying out the idea of playing two games simultaneously to see if it might be worth pursuing on other occasions (two such reports are quoted on page 28). Although there is nothing explicit in the surviving records to confirm whether this is the case – the Surrey minutes are surprisingly silent on the consequences and significance of the decision to play the home match with Oxford at the same time as a Championship Match, and of the attitude of the Committee Members towards doing so – this may perhaps be closer to the truth of the situation.

Summing up
So no, it wasn't an error, a muddle, or a mix-up that led to Surrey playing two simultaneous first-class matches in June 1909. It was the choice consciously made by the county club as a result of trying to fit too many matches into too tight a schedule, in a fixture list made more than usually crowded for Surrey by the visit of the Australians.

1909 was, perhaps, an opportunity for Surrey to give up gracefully their proud record of playing all their county opponents twice in every season since 1890, apart from in four seasons where special circumstances applied. But they chose not to do so. It was also an opportunity for them to loosen their strong ties with the Universities, had they wanted to do so. But they did not do this either.

Instead, Surrey in 1909 stood by a decision taken early in the fixture-making process to play all the other counties twice, and to play both Universities at home and away "if possible" – even if in doing so they stretched the limit of what was "possible" to a degree that some might now see as irrational.

Surrey themselves may perhaps have sought to rationalise this decision by allowing the whole thing to be regarded as an experiment, to see how the playing of two matches simultaneously might work out in practice; or perhaps as a way of testing the market for first-class cricket in the county away from The Oval - though why do that when 'the market' would inevitably have split loyalties if another, and as it turned out a better, county side was playing at The Oval at the same time?

But from the sources inspected, the conclusion must be that the double-header with Lancashire and Oxford University was simply the only way of accommodating the county club's insistence on playing Oxford University at home and away in 1909. That insistence could only be honoured by doubling up Surrey's fixtures on one occasion during the middle of the season – stretching the definition of what was "possible", but not, as a one-off, stretching it beyond breaking-point. Perhaps the reason that the minutes are silent about the doubling-up issue is that at the time it wasn't seen as anything particularly remarkable – it was just the way the county's fixture list turned out, given the self-imposed constraints upon it.

Whatever the reason, the decision was made: Surrey would play Oxford University twice during the season, and that meant having to play the home game away from The Oval and on dates when another county game had already been arranged. Now there were other details to sort out.

GETTING READY

Why Reigate?
Having decided that the Oxford University match would have to be played away from The Oval, Surrey CCC had to find another ground that could accommodate it. By this time, the county had played Second Eleven fixtures on three out-grounds – at Reigate Priory CC (which had hosted one Minor Counties match in each year from 1905 to 1908 inclusive), at Epsom CC (one Minor Counties match in 1906), and at Guildford Sports Ground (one Minor Counties match in 1908). These were presumably the leading candidates for the first-class fixture in 1909. I say 'presumably' because the surviving Surrey records do not say anything about the selection of the venue for the Oxford match. This is surprising, given that decisions about out-ground venues for Second XI fixtures were minuted for the 1906, 1908

and 1909 seasons[6] – though sadly not for 1905, so we have no definitive record as to why Reigate was chosen in that year as Surrey's first-ever out-ground.[7] In fact, neither the Match Committee nor the full Committee met between 15 October 1908, when the decision was taken to play the Oxford match away from The Oval, and the County Secretaries' meeting on 8 December, when the 1909 fixture list was agreed with the match allocated to Reigate. So we must assume that Surrey's decision to choose Reigate was taken outside the normal Committee processes – though even then it is surprising that the decision was not minuted somewhere, even if only to record that such a decision had been properly taken.

So once again, we are left to speculate as to why Reigate got the nod. The following are possible factors in the decision:

· When looking for out-grounds, Surrey CCC may have wanted to make a deliberate choice to use grounds outside metropolitan Surrey, in order to spread the game more widely through the county rather than looking to 'metropolitan' venues such as Croydon, Battersea, Richmond, Mitcham or even Kingston, all of which were by now part of or contiguous with London's built-up area, or were fast becoming so.

· Although nowadays we may think of Reigate as 'just another dormitory town' in Surrey, in the first decade of the 20th century it, with the adjoining town of Redhill, was comfortably the largest town in non-metropolitan Surrey. Thus holding the fixture at Reigate would make it accessible to the greatest number of people, with consequential benefits in terms of receipts as well as in more general proselytising.

· Reigate had a cricketing pedigree. Major matches in Reigate are reported as early as 1832, although big-name players from Reigate were known from half a century earlier. The Reigate Priory club was founded on its present site west of Bell Street in the mid-19th century - 1852 is the generally-accepted date, though club records are slightly ambiguous on the point.[8]

· Reigate was also the home town of Surrey star W.W. (Walter) Read, who was able to ensure that it retained a high cricketing profile. In 1893, 1894 and 1895 he arranged matches at the Priory club's ground in which his own XI opposed an XI brought together by W.G.Grace. Among those taking part in these matches were players of the quality of Bobby Abel, J.J.Ferris, Tom Hayward, J.T.Hearne, George Lohmann, Archie MacLaren, Billy Murdoch, Bobby Peel, Ranji, and Tom Richardson - and of course Read and W.G. themselves.

· In the last quarter of the 19th century, Reigate Priory CC had been making occasional noises in the hope of securing a full county fixture on

---

6   Minutes of Match Committee meetings on 20 December 1905, 21 February 1907, and 3 and 26 November 1908.

7   As noted earlier, all of Surrey's home First Eleven matches from 1854, and the first 90 home Second Eleven matches between July 1889 and August 1904, were played at The Oval. There is nothing in the Surrey minutes, or the relevant Yearbooks, that gives any background to the ground-breaking decision to play some Second XI matches away from The Oval in 1905.

8   One document seen at the club by the author suggests an alternative date of 1862.

their ground. Although financial factors were against them, their efforts may well have put them in prime position for consideration when venues away from The Oval were first being sought for Minor Counties matches in 1905, and later for a first-class fixture in 1909.[9]

· In the season before the first-ever county match at Reigate in 1905, the ground had had three examinations by some Very Important People in Surrey cricket. In July 1904 Reigate Priory CC played matches first against the Gentlemen of Surrey, whose team included W.T.Graburn who was the Surrey CCC coach from 1892 to 1904, and then two days later against Mr J.Shuter's XI; John Shuter had been Surrey's captain in their heyday of the 1880s and early 1890s and was still a major influence at The Oval, being (among other things) Chairman of the Match Committee. Then in September they played against Mr H.D.G.Leveson Gower's XII; 'Shrimp' Leveson Gower was a regular member of the Surrey XI (or as regular as most amateurs of the era) who went on to captain both Surrey and England, and after retiring as a player was a leading cricket administrator and organiser both in Surrey and nationally for the best part of 40 years. Thus the Reigate club was in a strong position to influence some very influential people in 1904, and to judge from subsequent events, they were very successful in doing so. The fact that the Leveson Gower family seat was nearby at Titsey can't have harmed the Reigate cause either.[10]

Whatever the balance among these factors, and perhaps others that we cannot now know, in late 1904 or early 1905 the Priory Ground at Park Lane was selected as the first home venue, other than The Oval, to host a Surrey First or Second Eleven match since 1854. The match – the first of the season for the Second XI – took place on 15-16 May 1905. It was welcomed locally, in principle at least, if not so much in terms of the attendance:

"It was an excellent idea – whoever was the originator of it – that one at least of Surrey's second eleven fixtures should be played in some part of the county[11], with a view of stimulating an interest in the game generally and in the county team especially.[12] Arising out of this idea Surrey 2nd and Yorkshire 2nd opened their season's campaign on Monday on the Reigate Priory Cricket Ground – one of the most picturesque spots obtainable. There was not a particularly large

9   For more on Walter Read's associations with the Priory club, and on the attempts by the club to secure a county match in the later 19th century, see Keith Booth: *Walter Read: A class act*, ACS Publications, 2011, especially pp. 24-31.

10   The proximity of his family seat may also have had a bearing on Leveson Gower's selection of the Priory CC ground for first-class matches by his own Eleven in 1924, 1934, 1935 and 1936, as noted on page 32 below. But strangely, he does not mention Reigate Priory CC in the chapter 'Cricket Clubs I Remember' in his autobiography *Off and On the Field* (1953).

11   Kennington Oval had been in the LCC area since 1889, and so was no longer in the administrative county of Surrey. It is not clear whether the newspaper was being a touch sarcastic here, or just using the term "the county" to mean "the non-metropolitan part of the geographical county".

12   I have speculated earlier that this may have been a factor in the decision to play matches outside metropolitan Surrey; but despite this reference in the newspaper I have traced nothing in Surrey's own records which corroborates the suggestion, plausible though it is, that this was a principal reason for playing away from London.

attendance, the numbers being slightly increased after lunch."

Surrey Mirror, Tuesday 16 May 1905

The experiment – if that is what it was – of playing a second eleven fixture at an out-ground away from the metropolitan area was evidently deemed a success, although in financial terms it was not lucrative.[13] The continuing pressures on The Oval led to Surrey repeating the venture for the next three seasons, with Reigate used in all three years: clearly it had not blotted its copybook over this period. As noted, by the end of the 1908 season grounds at Epsom and Guildford had also been used for Second Eleven matches, but when towards the end of that year the club was looking for an out-venue for the following season's first-class match against Oxford University, Reigate Priory CC had evidently retained its primacy.

There was perhaps one other factor in the confirmation of Reigate as the venue for the Oxford University match. Nearby Gatton Park was the home of Sir Jeremiah Colman, since 1885 the head of the Colman's mustard family. During his lifetime, Sir Jeremiah held numerous positions of power, both inside and outside cricket. As *Wisden* said, he had cricket in his blood, and applied "close interest and unflagging zeal" to the game. He became a member of the Surrey CCC Committee, and was President of the club from 1916 until 1922, and thereafter an enthusiastic Vice-President. He was also a friend of Reigate Priory CC, and was the club's President from 1909 until his death in 1942. Far be it from me to suggest that the choice of Reigate for the Oxford match was directly influenced by him or his presence in very senior Surrey circles, but - like the proximity of the Leveson Gower seat - it surely can't have done any harm to Reigate's chances.

Reigate: Anticipation and preparation

The coming of first-class cricket to Reigate does not appear to have raised great excitement in the local area. There is no mention of the fixture in the Reigate-based local newspaper, the *Surrey Mirror*, at any time in the last three months of 1908 when it was being arranged and confirmed, nor in early 1909 after the publication of the season's fixture list in *Wisden*. The earliest local reference that I have traced came in mid-April, when the *Mirror*'s columnist 'Sportsman' included this in his preview of Surrey's forthcoming season:

"My readers will be pleased to learn that the home engagement with the Dark Blues will be decided at Reigate, the exigencies of the programme being such that it will be decided simultaneously with the Lancashire contest at the Oval".

Cricket Prospects by 'Sportsman' in the Surrey Mirror, 13 April 1909

The local press then again fell silent on the subject until the eve of the match; of which more anon.

But as might be expected, excitement was greater at Reigate Priory CC. At

---

13   Figures of receipts for the 1905 match against Yorkshire II are unfortunately not available, but they are unlikely to have been much different from those for the following season's Second XI match against Lancashire II at Reigate, gate receipts for which were £7-9s-3d. Assuming an entry charge of 3d, this indicates a paying attendance over the two days of just under 600 non-club-members.

its AGM on 28 April 1909 the Club President reported that

"An attractive list of club fixtures has been arranged for the coming Season, and the Committee have pleasure in stating that the Surrey County Club has arranged for the First Class County Match, Surrey v Oxford University, to take place on the ground on June 21st, 22nd and 23rd".

No mention here of the simultaneous Lancashire match, for that might have dampened the enthusiasm somewhat!

The President's written report was, of course, just the bare bones. The *Surrey Mirror* reported in more detail the remarks that the President made when speaking to his report, and the comments made upon it by others:

"[The President, Mr J.Walters JP, remarked that] there were some very good fixtures for the coming season, and he believed the match with Oxford University was the first first-class county match to take place on the ground, and it was certainly a very great honour and should be of great advantage to them (hear hear). It was another proof of the great kindness of their friend, Mr H.D.G.Leveson Gower, and he hoped the match would be largely patronised. With regard to their expenditure, they had to spend the sum of £30 at least in repairing the pavilion, £10 of which would be kindly paid by the Surrey County Club, on condition that they spent £10 in addition. There were some other necessary repairs to be done, and he hoped when the public appreciated the advantages the Club was to the neighbourhood, they would come forward and subscribe more liberally to the funds. With the special attractions they had this year they sought to have a very successful season indeed (applause).

"Mr J.Nightingale seconded the motion, and remarked that although this would be the first time a first-class county match would be played at Reigate, it would not be the first time first-class cricket would have taken place there.[14] He hoped that the match, being a county fixture, would be well patronised by the town and district (hear hear)."
Surrey Mirror, 30 April 1909

The welcome given by the club to the fixture was to be expected, but evidently their facilities, though adequate for Second Eleven cricket for the previous four seasons, were not felt to be up to the standard appropriate to a first-class match. With this in mind, early in 1909 the Priory club approached Surrey CCC for a grant towards the improvement of their pavilion, and - not without some hesitation - a grant of £10 was duly made.[15] As the total cost of the improvements was close to £40, this could be seen as a pretty token effort on the county club's part; but perhaps it is unfair to seek to pass judgement on this today.

By mid-June 1909, all seemed to be ready for Reigate's first true first-class match. It was previewed in the *Surrey Mirror* on Friday 18 June. The paper was principally concerned with singing the praises of the expected Surrey XI, and having done so, its report concluded

---

14   This may have been true if the term "first class" is understood simply to mean "high quality", but it was not true in the strict cricketing use of the term.

15   Minutes of the Surrey CCC Match Committee 14 January 1909, and the full Committee on 18 February and 18 March 1909.

" ... with Oxford University stronger than they have been for years, the match should be productive of cricket worth going a long way to witness."

The hopes of Reigate Priory CC at their AGM, and of the *Surrey Mirror's* correspondent, for a good attendance were natural enough. But not all local cricket-lovers shared their excitement about the fixture, as evidenced by this letter which appeared in the same edition of the paper:

"Dear Sir – Though we are promised the opportunity to see "Surrey v Oxford University" at Reigate on Monday next, Surrey is playing Lancashire away from home that day![16] If the former is a 2nd XI, or Club and Ground fixture, why is it not advertised as such? Is this cricket? Yours etc, "HOW'S THAT", Reigate, June 16th."

As stated in the Introduction, the first-class status of the Reigate match has never been challenged, either at the time or subsequently, and its credentials as a first-class match are unimpeachable. Whether 'How's That', and any other residents of Reigate who shared his scepticism, ever accepted that fact we can never know.

Team selection

With the club having two first-class matches to play on 21-23 June 1909, Surrey's selectors had an interesting task on their hands in picking the two elevens. Yet again, primary sources on the subject are, infuriatingly, lacking (why is there no mention of the selection issue in the minutes of the Match Committee – especially given that it was chaired by one of those who played in the Reigate game?). So once more we are forced back on speculation and assumptions.

Selecting the side for the Lancashire match was no doubt straightforward. This was a Championship match, with points at stake, between two of the country's most senior county clubs who, at the time of the match, stood second (Surrey) and third (Lancashire) in the Championship table. In these circumstances there could be no question of trying to balance the two sides for the Oval and Reigate fixtures: the match at The Oval had to take priority. So the side for the Lancashire match was unquestionably the county's First XI, and showed only one change from the eleven that had drawn with Sussex at Horsham in the previous championship match. The selected XI was as follows – the figure in brackets is the number of first-team matches which they had already played this season (out of a maximum of 14 – i.e. 12 Championship games plus one match each against the Australians and Oxford University):

J.B.Hobbs (11), E.G.Hayes (13), A.Marshal (14), J.N.Crawford (14), H.S.Harrison (5), W.E.Davis (7), A.Ducat (12), H.D.G.Leveson Gower, captain (9), W.S.Lees (13), T.Rushby (9) and H. Strudwick (11).

Only two players who had played five matches or more were missing from this XI – Tom Hayward (who had played six matches, but was currently injured), and Bill Hitch, who had played seven matches, and was the player from the Horsham match who gave way to Rushby for the fixture at The Oval.

---

16   In fact the Lancashire match was at The Oval.

The interesting part was the choice of the side to play Oxford University. On the face of it, the prime candidates might have been thought to be those who had already played for the First XI during the season, together with any others who had appeared in the three Second Eleven fixtures that had been played so far. On this basis, the candidates would have been those set out here:

First and Second XI appearances for Surrey in 1909 prior to 21 June
(excluding players selected for Surrey v Lancashire on that date)

	For 1st XI (max 14)	For 2nd XI (max 3)	Style	Specialism (at the time)
W.J.Abel	--	3	RHB, RFM/LBG	Opening batsman
H.S.Altham	1	--	RHB, RM	Batsman
H.G.Blacklidge	--	3	LHB, LFM/SLA	All-rounder
W.J.H.Curwen	4	--	RHB, RFM	Batsman; occ bowler
F.Edwards	1	2	LHB, LM/SLA	Bowler
E.G.Goatly	3	1	RHB, SLA	Batsman; occ bowler
T.W.Hayward	6	--	RHB, RM	Opening batsman
J.W.Hitch	7	--	RHB, RF	Fast bowler; hitter
M.T.Jackson	--	1	LHB, LM	Bowler
J.E.V.Jewell	--	2	not known	Opening batsman
E.C.Kirk	3	--	LHB, LMF	Bowler
E.B.Myers	--	2	RHB, SLA	Batsman; occ bowler
G.J.W.Platt	--	3	RHB, RM/OB	Bowler
A.W.F.Rutty	--	3	RHB, OB	Batsman; 2nd XI captain
W.C.Smith	4	--	RHB, OB	Bowler
W.A.Spring	4	3	RHB, RFM	All-rounder
A.U.Udal	--	2	not known	Bowler
H.E.Vigar	3	3	RHB, WK	Wicket-keeper
C.T.A.Wilkinson	1	2	RHB, SLA	Batsman; occ bowler

However, few of those who had already turned out for the First XI had covered themselves with glory in the season so far. This was particularly true of the batsmen: between them, Harry Altham, Wilfred Curwen, Edward Goatly, William Spring and Cyril Wilkinson had had 20 innings for the First XI in 1909 for a combined average of 7.45, with only four double-figure innings between them and a highest innings of 28, by Altham. At least Goatly had some longer-term pedigree, having been an occasional member of the First XI since 1903, and having a first-class century to his name (147* v Derbyshire at The Oval in 1905): but he was regarded as a player whose early promise had not been fulfilled, and he was, to put it kindly, not a lively fielder.

Some of the bowlers had done rather better. Bill Hitch had 32 wickets at 20.93 from his seven first team matches, as well as playing an innings of 45; Frank Edwards had taken 3-31 on his first-class debut against Oxford

University early in the season; and 'Razor' Smith had 25 wickets at 8.72 from just four matches, including 11-52 against Worcestershire at The Oval. Smith had also played an innings of 201 in Surrey's previous competitive game at Reigate, the Minor Counties match against Buckinghamshire in August 1908. Surely all three of these bowlers would be contenders for the Reigate side?

Turning to the Second XI players, there was fortunately a bit more form to encourage the selectors, even though there were no outstanding claims. William Abel, Arthur Rutty (a former Oxford student) and Spring had all made scores in the 60s in the three Second Eleven matches so far[17], while Wilkinson had a 46*, and George Platt had taken six wickets in the match against Lancashire II. There had also been some good performances in Club & Ground games in the early part of the season. Abel had taken 20 wickets in the eight (mostly single-innings) matches in which he had bowled, and he made scores of 78 and 65 in matches at The Oval on 17 and 18 June, against Sutton and Battersea respectively. Goatly's batting had been even more successful, including scores of 170*, 94 and 71 in his seven C&G matches to date (the 71 and 170* again coming on 17 and 18 June). Platt had taken 29 wickets in his first eight C&G matches of the season, including innings returns of 7-26 and 6-30; and Spring had hit 45 and 88* in one (two-innings) match early in June. Like Razor Smith, Spring also had 'form' at Reigate, having performed the match double there when he scored 102 and took 6-44 and 4-50 for Surrey II in a Minor Counties match against Berkshire in June 1907.

On this evidence, the likeliest candidates for a place in the side at Reigate might have been perhaps Abel, Platt, Spring, Goatly, Hitch and Smith – though had Abel's and Goatly's performances on 17 and 18 June come too late to impress the selectors? Other contenders might have been Rutty (the established Second XI captain) and maybe Henry Blacklidge, who had been a steady performer for the Second XI in 1907 and 1908, together with the established second-choice wicket-keeper Herbert Vigar.

But there were other considerations too. A match against Oxford University might be an opportunity to call in some amateurs, especially those with Oxford connections. And as the game was going to a cricketing 'outpost', was there perhaps some local player who might be worth a run out in the side, to create some additional local interest (and additional revenue)? And as this was to be a first-class match, would a side made up of players who could not establish themselves in the First XI – or in many cases, could not even break into the First XI – be strong enough to give a good account of themselves, and thus to maintain Surrey's reputation?

No doubt these factors all had a part to play in the decision to search wider for potential players for the Reigate match, and in the final team selection. But quite what possessed **John Shuter**[18] – Chairman of the Match Committee, remember, so he was in the best position to influence these

---

17   The three matches played so far were against the Second Elevens of Lancashire, Kent and Yorkshire. None counted towards the Minor Counties championship, which was being played on a regional basis this year.

18   Those eventually selected for the Surrey side at Reigate are named in bold type in the following paragraphs.

things – to select himself as captain for the Reigate match cannot now be ascertained. Arthur Rutty's credentials for captaining the side were passed over in favour of those of a man who was 54 years and 132 days old at the start of the match, and who had played no first-class cricket for 16 years (and only one major match in the meantime, a non-first-class game for Surrey against the West Indian tourists in 1900). The *Surrey Mirror* reported on 18 June that Shuter "has been indulging in a tremendous lot of club cricket lately, and is very fit" – though I have to say that his name does not appear in any of the club cricket scores printed in *Cricket* in the earlier part of 1909, and neither had he turned out even once in Club & Ground matches. We may surmise that Shuter's aim in selecting himself was twofold – to provide some experience in what was otherwise likely to be a relatively inexperienced side, and as a sentimental gesture designed to make the fixture more attractive, in the absence of Surrey's 'big name' drawcards who were all playing at The Oval.

Two of the three past or future Test cricketers from the Surrey side at Reigate were John Shuter (left), who played his last match for Surrey in this game, and Morice Bird, who was making his debut for the county. (Both photos courtesy of Surrey CCC)

The shortage of experienced and in-form batsmen among the contenders from the season's First and Second Elevens could perhaps excuse the selectors for looking elsewhere to fill some of the places in the top half of the order. The four who were selected were all amateurs, two of whom had an Oxford connection.

Morice Bird, Liverpool-born but Surrey-qualified, had first made his name by scoring a century in each innings for Harrow against Eton in 1907 (still a unique achievement in that fixture, and likely to remain so, as for many years this match has been played as a one-day, single-innings fixture). He had played three first-class matches already in 1909 – one for MCC and two for Leveson Gower's XI – scoring 51 for MCC v Leicestershire, and then a fine 137 for Leveson Gower's XI against Cambridge University on 11 June. Here at least was a batsman in form. **Harry Altham** was a rather different pick. He had played once for Surrey's First XI in 1908, and later in that season he had scored 132 for Surrey II against Berkshire in a Minor Counties match; he had also made one First XI appearance earlier in 1909. He was now in his first year at Oxford University, but had not established a place in the University's First XI. The Reigate fixture provided an opportunity to further the career of this promising batsman, and a good performance against his University colleagues might help him towards a Blue.

If there was some recent(ish) form to go on when selecting these two batsmen, the same could not easily be said of the other two 'outsiders' who found favour for the Reigate fixture. **William Sarel** had played three first-class matches for Surrey in 1904, none of them in the Championship, scoring 44 and 12 against Cambridge University but making only 1, 1, 1 and 4 in his other four innings. A soldier, he had spent some of the intervening time on his duties in Trinidad, where he had played four first-class matches in which his highest scores were two more innings in the 40s. But with a career average of 17.92 to his name, and no first-class cricket since January 1906, it is difficult to see what exactly he was expected to bring to the side at Reigate. **John Raphael** came to the match not long after fighting a losing battle for the Liberals in a Parliamentary by-election at Croydon. He had played for Oxford University from 1903 to 1905, scoring 201 against Yorkshire in 1904, and was a fairly regular member of the Surrey First XI from 1904 until mid-1906, when he disappeared from county cricket for ever, apart from the Reigate match. Perhaps it was an innings of 113 for the Free Foresters in a non-first-class match against Oxford University in June 1908 that had kept him in Surrey's mind? He had also made his mark on the rugby field, playing in nine internationals for England as a three-quarter between 1902 and 1906.

Were these the best amateurs that Surrey could find? As well as Oxford-educated Second XI captain Arthur Rutty[19], there were two others around who had connections with both Surrey and Oxford University, and who might possibly have been in the selectors' minds. Hugh Teesdale had won his Blue at Oxford in 1908 and played one match for Surrey in each of 1906 and 1908; after his final first-class match in 1910 his career average was just over 30. Harry Chinnery had played for the Oxford University Authentics on tour in India in 1902/03, and played 30 matches for Surrey between 1897 and 1904; his final career record was 2536 runs at just under 25, but he had played no first-class cricket since 1904. Both might have had at least as good a claim to a place in the side at Reigate as some of those who were selected, but it is fair to say that neither of them had any credentials which placed them clearly ahead of those who finally made the Reigate XI.

---

19   Rutty had not played first-class cricket at Oxford, despite useful performances with bat and ball in the Seniors Matches in 1893 and 1894 – he scored 78 in the 1893 match, and took a hat-trick in 1894. He eventually made his one and only first-class appearance for Surrey v Oxford University in 1910, batting at number 10, scoring 12* and 6*, not bowling, and taking one catch.

Other possibles might perhaps have been former Surrey captains Lord Dalmeny (last match for Surrey 1908) and Digby Jephson (last match 1904), as well as two recently-retired pros, Albert Baker (now playing in Ireland) and Frederick Holland; and not forgetting Harry Bush, who played for Surrey from 1901 to 1912, but was frequently absent on military duty. Neither should we forget up-and-coming youngsters who were to break through to the First XI over the next couple of years – players like 18-year-old Ion Campbell from Repton School, or Tokyo-born Julian Piggott, now in his second year at Cambridge where he had performed well enough in the Freshman's and Seniors matches without getting a first-team place (though it was surely inconceivable that a Cambridge undergraduate would have been selected for a county fixture against Oxford). And a few months earlier there had been a missed opportunity regarding a youngster named Andrew Sandham[20] ...

Without knowing who was approached, and why, it is difficult to comment on the soundness of the selection of the non-groundstaff batsmen for the Reigate game. Perhaps, strange though their selections may now seem, Sarel, Raphael – yes, and Shuter too – were genuinely the best available.

As for the 'local selection', there was an obvious candidate in **Harry Budgen**, a slow left-arm bowler who had been a member of Reigate Priory CC since 1902. Budgen had played once for Surrey in 1904 (he was selected after taking six wickets for Reigate Priory against the Gentlemen of Surrey, and then 8-115 in an innings against John Shuter's XI, both in July 1904), and once again in 1905, though he had gone wicketless on both occasions.[21] In 1904 he had taken 140 wickets for the Priory club at 12.87 – over three times as many as any of the club's other bowlers - and in a reduced 1905 season he took 55 wickets at 10.80. Figures for later seasons are unfortunately not available, but his fame had gone before him, locally at least: speaking to its local audience, the *Surrey Mirror* wrote, when puffing the Surrey team for the forthcoming Oxford game, that "the record

Reigate's own: Harry Budgen

of H Budgen in local cricket is too well known to need any reference in these columns" (*Surrey Mirror* 18 June 1909).

---

20   From the minutes of the Match Committee, 10 September 1908: "The question of engaging Sandham of Streatham and Blythe of Kent on the Ground Staff in 1909 was considered. The Committee do not consider their engagement desirable." Two 'What might have beens' for the price of one! Sandham had turned 18 in July 1908; it was 1911 before he finally broke through on to the Surrey staff.

21   According to the *Surrey Mirror*, Budgen had come close to joining those taking a wicket with their first ball in first-class cricket, but after that his debut match seems to have gone downhill: "The young Reigate Priory player, H.Budgen ... was given a trial in the Surrey team [against Nottinghamshire], and received the honour of going in fifth wicket down. Over-eagerness, perhaps, led to his early dismissal [he was run out for 2], and later in the day, after beating and nearly bowling W.Gunn with his first ball, was rather ineffective" [*Surrey Mirror*, 2 August 1904].

To the six players just highlighted, the selectors added the amateur Wilfred Curwen and the professionals William Abel, Edward Goatly, George Platt, Herbert Vigar (another local man: his club cricket was for Redhill), Bill Hitch, William Spring and Henry Blacklidge, giving a squad of 14 from whom the final selection was to be made. The squad was selected before 18 June, for it was announced in the *Surrey Mirror* on that date, indicating that Abel's and Goatly's performances in the Club & Ground match on that date were not factors in their selection – not for the squad, at least.

So there was no place in the squad for Razor Smith, nor was there a sentimental or appreciative pick for Rutty. Both played for Surrey Club & Ground against Norwood on 22 June (the second day of the Reigate match), so it seems unlikely that they missed selection for the Reigate game through injury.[22]

The *Mirror* said on 18 June that
"It has been definitely decided that the seven amateurs [Shuter, Bird, Altham, Sarel, Raphael, Budgen and Curwen] will play, and the remaining four places will be filled from the seven professionals whose names are given above [Abel, Blacklidge, Goatly, Hitch, Pratt, Spring and Vigar]."

Six of the seven amateurs were essentially batsmen (the exception being Budgen); add in a wicket-keeper and there would be room for only three professional bowlers. So it is unsurprising that the two specialist bowlers among the listed professionals, **Hitch** and **Platt**, were both selected for the final eleven, Hitch providing the only real pace in the attack.

In the event, for reasons unknown (perhaps because of the balance of the side?) one of the amateurs, Curwen, did not play, so only two of the remaining professionals had to be omitted. As **Abel** and **Goatly** could both bowl respectably, and moreover had both shown excellent recent form in the Club & Ground fixtures on 17 and 18 June, they must have been seen as the natural choices to play, along with wicket-keeper **Vigar**. Blacklidge and Spring were accordingly the ones who drew the short straws.

The final Surrey XI for the match at Reigate was thus as follows. The numbers in brackets are the numbers of first-class matches which they had played in their careers to date, and the number played to date in 1909: W.J.Abel (0, 0), H.S.Altham (4, 3), M.C.Bird (15, 4), H.Budgen (2, 0), E.G.Goatly (52, 3), J.W.Hitch (27, 7), G.J.W.Platt (5, 0), J.E.Raphael (88, 0), W.G.M.Sarel (6, 0), J.Shuter (305, 0), and H.E.Vigar (8, 3).

The chosen side was a definite mix of youth and age, of callowness and experience. There were three players under the age of 22 (Altham 20y 7m, Bird 21:3 and Abel 21:10), and three over the age of 30 (Budgen 30:2, Sarel 33:6, and Shuter 54:4). Abel was the only one with no prior first-class experience, though five of his team-mates had played fewer than 10 first-class games, and only five had had any first-class experience in 1909.

---

22   Smith's appearances for Surrey up to this date had been limited by the fact that, rightly or otherwise, he was seen purely as a wet-weather bowler. Nevertheless, his non-selection when Surrey had to pick two first-class elevens seems difficult to explain. Perhaps he was squeezed out of the Reigate game by the home-town selection of Budgen?

Only three had played as many as 30 first-class matches (the equivalent of one full county season), and only Shuter had had a career of any real length – and even that had to all intents and purposes ended 16 years previously. This may have been virtually as strong a side as Surrey could put out for this fixture, given that there was another match at The Oval (though if Hayward had been able to turn out despite his lameness, and if Razor Smith had not been overlooked for whatever reason, it would surely have been stronger). But it was hardly one to put the fear of heavy defeat into their opponents.

A Surrey squad of 1908, including two of those who played at Reigate the following year, and six who played in the simultaneous match at The Oval. Standing, l to r: H.G.Blacklidge, A.Ducat, G.J.W.Platt, A.Marshal, J.W.Hitch, H.Strudwick, F.Boyington (scorer); seated: E.G.Hayes, J.B.Hobbs, H.D.G.Leveson Gower, T.W.Hayward, F.C.Holland. (Courtesy of Surrey CCC)

PLAY!
The following descriptions of play are taken principally from the contemporary reports in the Manchester Guardian, The Times, the edition of 'Cricket' dated 24 June 1909, and the Reigate-based Surrey Mirror. Complete scorecards of the two matches are included on pages 38 and 39.

Day 1 – Monday 21 June 1909
At both The Oval and Reigate the weather when the games started was dull and cool, with conditions forecast to get worse as the matches progressed. Both the visiting sides won the toss and chose to bat, and both took full advantage.

At The Oval the biggest crowd of the season so far was in attendance - not surprising for a match between the sides currently second and third in the Championship. They saw Lancashire bat until twenty minutes before the close, when they were all out for 343, made at a respectable 3.3 runs per over. Star of the show was Jack Sharp, who should have been stumped off the bowling of Ernie Hayes when he had made only 8, but went on to a dominating 157, scored in around 3½ hours with 14 fours. His runs were made out of a reported 237 added while he was at the crease - although this does not tally with the generally-accepted fall of wicket details, which indicate a figure of 246. This innings confirmed Sharp's fine early-season form, and no doubt contributed to his selection for his Test debut at Headingley ten days later.

Nine of the ten Lancashire wickets were taken by players now thought of more as batsmen, though both were regular bowlers too: Hayes' leg-breaks brought him 5-94 (his first five-wicket haul since May 1906), while Alan Marshal's fast-medium brought him 4-56 (his best innings figures of a season in which he took just 22 wickets).

With ten minutes of play remaining, Surrey began their first innings with, in effect, two night-watchmen – the captain Leveson Gower and wicket-keeper Strudwick. It was an eventful ten minutes. Fast bowler Walter Brearley, who had earlier played a belligerent innings of 26, seems to have been in a similar mood with the ball, for after Leveson Gower had scored the first two runs off the bat of the Surrey innings, he was "badly hit on the hand by a ball from Mr Brearley and had to retire" (*The Times*). This brought the day's proceedings to a slightly premature close, with Surrey on 4-0.

Given the threatening weather forecast, it was probably 'Advantage Lancashire' after Day 1, but at least Surrey had all their principal batsmen intact for the morning.

Meanwhile 20 miles away at Reigate, Oxford's batsmen had been making hay even more rapidly against Surrey's limited attack. Before an attendance described in the *Surrey* Mirror as 'disappointing', local boy Harry Budgen was given the honour of bowling the first over, but it was not until after lunch that the first breakthrough was made. Malcolm Salter, 97* at lunch, went to his maiden century (out of 143) soon after, and was eventually caught at mid-on off Morice Bird, the seventh bowler tried by Surrey. Salter's 152 included 18 fours, and came in 220 minutes.

Soon after his dismissal Arnold Seitz reached his own maiden century, after two hours' batting. His dismissal for 120, made in 135 minutes with 21 fours, gave Harry Budgen his first-ever first-class wicket, in his third match and nearly five years after his debut.

By now Oxford had already passed the total that Lancashire were to reach in almost the full day at The Oval, but there was plenty more to come. Vigorous batting from the University captain Christopher Hurst (whose stand with Charles Hooman added 53 in 20 minutes) and left-hander Richard Sale took the score along ever more rapidly, and close of play came with Oxford in the healthy position of 465-6. By the end of the day Hooman (73*) was reportedly "flogging the tired bowling to his heart's content". At both The Oval and Reigate, Surrey's fielding had deteriorated as the day went on, with chances being missed at both grounds.

Day 2 – Tuesday 22 June 1909

The forecast rain came overnight on 21/22 June, and conditions for the second day at The Oval and at Reigate were very different from those on the previous day. At The Oval the rain "rob[bed] the wicket of much of its previous perfection" (*Manchester Guardian*), while at Reigate there were still threatening clouds overhead when play resumed. At each ground, the early part of the day went relatively well for the batting side, but this time things fell apart in both games as the day went on.

At The Oval, the damage to Leveson Gower had been diagnosed as a broken finger, and he could take no further part in the match. The resumed first-wicket partnership was in the hands of the unlikely pairing of Strudwick and Hobbs, and although Strudwick left at 42 and Hobbs at 77, the innings progressed without undue alarms until the score reached 126-3; at which point the roof fell in, as four wickets fell for the addition of only two more runs. Worse followed when Lees's brief but eventful innings came to an early end: "Lees received four balls from Brearley, each of which struck him, and then retired hurt, owing to a severe blow on the hand" (*Cricket*). When the eighth wicket fell at 159, still 35 short of the target for avoiding the follow-on, the innings ended with Ducat as Brearley's fourth victim, or sixth if you include his part in the two 'retired hurts'. The innings had lasted just 2½ hours.

The follow-on was enforced, and Surrey's second innings began in sunshine. But their position was "hopeless" (*Cricket*) and "they never looked like saving the game" (*Manchester Guardian*). Only Harrison, Hayes and Ducat offered prolonged resistance, with Ducat's batting described in the *Guardian as* " the best of all ... he played so easily as to make it apparent that the wicket was not really so difficult as to make a fighting score impossible". But the other specialist batsmen contributed little, the tail did not wag, and with only nine men fit to bat Surrey were all out for 149, so losing inside two days by an innings and 35 runs. For Lancashire, fast-bowler Brearley had taken nine wickets in the match, as well as knocking two other Surrey players out of the game. But Surrey could not blame their poor batting performances on being short-handed, as neither of the injured players (Leveson Gower and Lees) was a front-line batsman.

There was not much comfort for Surrey from this comprehensive defeat. Contemporary reports acknowledged that Lancashire had had the best of the luck, in terms of the toss, the weather, the pitch, and the injuries to two Surrey players. But "even allowing for their luck Lancashire played a winning game throughout and thoroughly deserved their victory" (*Manchester Guardian*); or in the words of a perhaps less locally-biased publication they "made every use of their opportunities and deserved to win" (*Cricket*). Their win, and Surrey's defeat, meant that the two sides swapped places in the Championship table, with Lancashire moving up to second place and Surrey slipping to third.

On Day 2 at Reigate, things did not go much better for the other Surrey team. Oxford batted on, and Hooman, who had scored his maiden first-class century in his previous innings, became the side's third century-maker before being dismissed for 117, made in 2½ hours and including two fives (the equivalent of sixes today) and 17 fours. The University were finally all out for 577, with debutant le Couteur still there on 53*. At the time this was their fourth-highest-ever innings total in a first-class match, the highest of all being 651 against Sussex at Hove in 1895. The latter remains their record, and since 1909 they have surpassed 577 on only two further occasions, once in 1921 and once in 2005.

For Surrey, three bowlers each took three wickets – Budgen and two of the less specialist bowlers, Abel and Bird. Their one genuine first-team-squad bowler, Bill Hitch, ended with the unhappy figures of 0-131.

Although Abel left early, Surrey's first innings reached 46-1 before they lost three wickets (Bird, Goatly and Altham) while adding only 15 more runs. Sarel however was showing "excellent form", and he and Raphael took the score past 100 without further loss. Sarel brought up his maiden first-class half-century with "a pretty leg-glance for four" before Raphael fell for 31 with the score at 124. Sarel himself went for 57 ten runs later, and wickets fell steadily thereafter to see Surrey all out for 191. Batting at number nine, 54-year-old John Shuter hit 18 with four fours and a two, while local hero Harry Budgen "played excellent cricket", and when he was finally the last man out he "was warmly applauded for his contribution of 25 – the third highest recorded by his side".

As at The Oval, enforcing the follow-on was a formality, and Surrey batted again 386 runs in arrears. It was soon clear that they were not going to be able to make a decent fight of it. Their batting order was substantially altered but to no avail, as four wickets fell quickly, and there was to be no way back from 10-4. When the seventh wicket fell at 91, Surrey seemingly were on their way to as quick a defeat as was being experienced by the senior side at The Oval. Indeed, at this point it was agreed to play on until 7pm instead of the usual 6.30, "in the hope of finishing the match that evening" (*Cricket*).[23]

But the tail wagged. Budgen once again stood firm, and he and Goatly added a further 60 runs before play was concluded for the day, with no further loss. Surrey were still 235 runs behind, and although defeat looked inevitable, at least the Surrey XI at Reigate - unlike its Oval counterpart - had managed to extend the game into its final day.

Day 3 – Wednesday 23 June 1909

The Reigate weather was not to come to Surrey's rescue. Play resumed on time, and the overnight partnership was quickly broken when Budgen left without adding to his overnight score of 30. Vigar joined Goatly and "vigorous cricket was witnessed", with 47 runs added in 25 minutes before Goatly was caught behind for 69, Surrey's top score of the match. 211-9, still 175 runs behind; but still Surrey would not lie down. Bill Hitch came in at number 11, perhaps still smarting after his expensive nought-for in Oxford's innings. Although bowling was his speciality, he was renowned as a hitter, and he lived up to that reputation today as he "hit out with great vigour in all directions". His 50 came up in only 30 minutes, and was the second maiden first-class 50 by a Surrey player in the match. But ten minutes later it was all over when he was caught off le Couteur's leg-spin for 59, made in 40 minutes out of a last-wicket stand of 77.

Surrey had been beaten by an innings and 98 runs, but the resistance offered for their last three wickets did credit to the players concerned.

---

23 'Hope' may not quite be the right word as far as Surrey were concerned, but we know what they mean!

Their efforts at least ensured that the defeat was nothing like as big as had seemed likely when the seventh wicket went down, and belied the lack of confidence shown in them when the hours of play were extended on the previous evening.

But could any of the Surrey players take any real satisfaction from the match? Well, surely Harry Budgen could – playing on his home ground he took his first three first-class wickets, scored 25 and 30, and was one of only three Surrey players to achieve double-figures in both innings. William Abel perhaps also took satisfaction from making his first-class debut and taking three wickets, even if his scores of 4 and 4 were not what he might have hoped for from his principal skill. And the two 'unexpected amateurs', Sarel and Raphael, let no-one down, Sarel top-scoring in the first innings, and Raphael reaching 30 in both innings.

Perhaps Goatly too took satisfaction from his 69 in a losing cause - and maybe more importantly to him, from the fact that it earned him a recall to the Championship XI for the next fixture. And maybe John Shuter enjoyed playing a first-class match again after 16 years, even though his scores of 18 and 1 meant a minute decrease in his final career average (from 21.31 to 21.26, if you must know!) But more generally the Reigate match was probably just regarded by the Surrey players as best forgotten: one to put down to experience.

AFTER THE EVENT

Immediate post mortems, and longer-term consequences

The immediate reaction to Surrey's double-header concentrated only on its success in cricketing terms, and not on whether the venture had achieved any other successes – which perhaps tells its own story:

> "It cannot be said that Surrey's experiment of playing two first-class matches simultaneously[24] met with much success, seeing that each team suffered a heavy reverse. The county gave a very disappointing display at the Oval ... [no further comment on the Reigate game]."
>
> Pavilion Gossip, in *Cricket: A weekly record of the game*, 24 June 1909

> "Surrey will look back upon the past week with anything but pleasant recollections. The experiment of playing two first-class matches on the same day was hardly a success, and the dual defeat of the county will not encourage its repetition."
>
> Sporting Notes, in *Surrey Mirror*, 29 June 1909

Whether the *Surrey Mirror* had more than just the results in mind when concluding that the 'experiment' was "hardly a success" is not clear, though the reference in the paper's Day 1 report that "attendance during the day was disappointing" was perhaps also in their minds.

Perhaps we can also read a lack of success into what was *not* said at the AGM of Reigate Priory CC in the spring of 1910. One might have expected some expression of satisfaction, not to say pleasure or even pride, from the club following the hosting of its first first-class match. But in contrast

---

24   Note the contemporary references here, and in the following quotation, to the first-class status of both games, and to the experimental nature of the double-header venture.

to the AGM report from twelve months previously, the report of the 1910 AGM in the *Surrey Mirror* makes no direct reference at all to the Oxford University match. After recording that it was reported to the AGM that £38-19s-2d had been spent in the year on "special improvements" to the pavilion and ground, and that Reigate Priory CC thanked Surrey CCC for their £10 grant towards this expenditure, the newspaper report continued:

> "The President [Sir Jeremiah Colman] remarked that he thought there was evidence ... that the gentlemen who were associated with county cricket were taking an interest in the organisation [i.e. in Reigate Priory CC]. Mr Leveson Gower had been very good in bringing teams down to Reigate, and the club owed him a debt of gratitude for doing so. As a member of the Surrey County Committee he could say that the committee did what it could to encourage cricket in the county, and the Reigate club had received some of that encouragement."

Surrey Mirror, 22 April 1910

And that's all. The silence on the Oxford University match is deafening, and the rest smacks to me rather of damning Surrey CCC with very faint praise.

When Surrey produced their accounts for the 1909 season, the disappointing financial return from the double-header – and particularly from the Reigate match – was there for all to see. The receipts from their home matches against the other 15 counties, all at The Oval of course, ranged between about £38 for the game against Gloucestershire (when there was play on the third day only) to £639 for the August Bank Holiday game against Notts, with an average of just under £213-14s. Receipts from the Lancashire match at The Oval were a reasonable-enough £274-1s-6d. Only the Middlesex and Notts matches earned more, and of course the Lancashire game only lasted two days.

But the receipts from the Oxford University game at Reigate were a mere £15-5s-6d.[25] These were far and away the lowest receipts from any of Surrey's first-class matches in 1909, and were closely on a par with those from each of the four Second Eleven matches played at The Oval (receipts from these four games totalled £61-0s-6d, the equivalent of £15-5s-1½d each). In terms of the balance-sheet, the expenses of £135-3s-2d incurred for the Reigate match meant that the fixture lost the club almost £120. Three home county matches during the season lost more: the Gloucestershire game lost £139, that against Derbyshire – played when Surrey's stars were involved in the Edgbaston Test against Australia – lost £127, and the Worcestershire game – when there was no play on the second day – lost £122. But none incurred so high a loss for so little income.

Perhaps by 1909 the Universities were not such a big draw as most county sides, but at least when Surrey had played them at The Oval in recent years the financial returns had been nowhere near as poor as they were from the Reigate fixture. The table below shows that between 1898 and 1908, Surrey's ten home fixtures with Oxford University had brought in receipts of between around £52 in 1907 (a rain-spoiled draw, with little play on

---

25   This is the equivalent of 611 paying customers over the three days of the game, assuming entry to be at a uniform 6d per person. Members of the Surrey and Reigate Priory clubs were admitted free.

the second day) and £167 in 1898, with an average of about £103. So the drop to not much more than £15 in 1909 was very striking. And over the same period, the ten fixtures had brought about five net profits, ranging between £3-7s and over £81, and five net losses, ranging between about £4-10s and almost £45. The net loss of almost £120 on the Reigate fixture in 1909 - on an expenditure that had climbed steeply compared with that of the preceding years - was surely not what had been looked for.

Surrey v Oxford University:
Expenses and receipts for matches in Surrey, 1898-1909

	Expenses			Receipts			Profit/Loss		
	£	s	d	£	s	d	£	s	d
1898	86	3	0	167	10	6	+ 81	7	6
1900	67	13	0	72	7	2	+ 4	14	2
1901	148	19	4	133	5	10	- 15	3	6
1902	129	12	10	90	9	0	- 39	3	10
1903	146	16	4	101	16	8	- 44	19	8
1904	67	5	6	115	1	0	+ 47	15	6
1905	91	10	0	94	17	10	+ 3	7	10
1906	89	3	0	121	7	8	+ 32	4	8
1907	86	2	9	51	17	6	- 34	5	3
1908	86	5	0	81	15	10	- 4	9	2
1909	135	3	2	15	5	6	- 119	17	8

As with Reigate Priory CC before them, when the report and accounts for 1909 were placed before Surrey's AGM early in 1910, there was a deafening silence in the Secretary's Report about the Reigate and double-header 'experiments'. It is probably not unreasonable to surmise that both ventures – that is, the decision to play a home match away from The Oval, and the separate but overlapping decision to play two matches at the same time – were now seen as something of an embarrassment, best passed over hastily in the review of the year.

Whether that surmise is true or not, when it came to deciding on the fixtures for 1910 there is no suggestion in the surviving records that Surrey ever contemplated repeating either venture. And although it had hosted one Second Eleven match in each season between 1905 and 1909, Reigate had now even lost its primacy in looking for grounds for Second Eleven matches - indeed, it was no better than sixth choice:

> "It was decided to play Second Eleven matches at Croydon, Guildford and Horley in 1910."
>
> *Minutes of SCCC Match Committee meeting of 21 October 1909*

... supplemented a month later by:

> "It was decided to play Second Eleven matches on the grounds of the Merton and Richmond clubs, or failing either of these, on the Reigate Priory ground."
>
> *Minutes of SCCC Match Committee meeting of 30 November 1909* [26]

---

26   The inclusion of Croydon, Merton and Richmond in these lists for 1910 indicates that it was no longer - if it ever had been - a priority that fixtures that could not be accommodated at The Oval should be played away from metropolitan Surrey.

In the end, four Second Eleven matches in 1910 were played at The Oval, with one at each of Horley, Guildford, and Merton – and Reigate. But Reigate was dropped from the Second Eleven fixture list for 1911 when the county decided on financial grounds to reduce its programme of Second Eleven matches, leaving Merton and Horley as the only out-grounds used in that year. From 1912 all home Second Eleven matches were once again played at The Oval, and apart from single matches at Richmond in 1923 and at Guildford in 1931 and 1934, that remained the case until these fixtures once again started being spread around the county in 1948.

After the Minor Counties match against Hertfordshire in August 1910, it was over 50 years before the Reigate Priory ground was used again by Surrey CCC. They eventually returned there 1962 for a Second Eleven fixture against Sussex II, as they also did in 1964 and 1965. The ground then once again fell out of favour, and was not used by Surrey again until 2006, since when one Second Eleven Championship match was arranged at the ground in each year to 2012, together with one match in the Second Eleven Trophy competition in 2006 and another (unfortunately abandoned without a ball bowled) in 2012.

Surrey still return to Reigate Priory CC for occasional Second Eleven matches. Here they are batting against Somerset II in a Second Eleven Championship match in May 2012.

We should also look briefly at the other issue which led to Surrey's double-header in 1909 – fixture pressures on The Oval.

There were no first-class tourists visiting England in 1910, and so the pressures that had been experienced on the ground the previous year were eased. As a result, Surrey were able to continue their series of home matches against Oxford University, as well as maintaining their full set of home and away fixtures against all the other counties - in both cases, without leaving The Oval for the home games. There was also room in the fixture list to play both Universities in away matches.

In 1911 the non-Test tour by All-India again meant that The Oval was not in demand to the same extent as in 1909. This time it was Cambridge's turn to play at The Oval, and once again Surrey were able to play all the other counties at home without leaving Kennington, as well as fitting in away fixtures against all counties and the two Universities.

But things came to a crunch in 1912. The visits of both Australia and South Africa for the Triangular Tournament – for both of whom a full county programme was also arranged - meant that the Surrey club was faced with a clear, if perhaps unpalatable, choice. With one Test match to fit in at The Oval as well as two county fixtures against each of the tourists, an early-season Test Trial, and a late-season (and late-arranged) fixture between a combined Surrey and Middlesex XI and the Australians, Surrey CCC concluded that they could not fit in matches at The Oval against all the other 15 counties together with one or both of the Universities. The choice was therefore to forfeit their proud record of achieving a 'full set' of county fixtures for longer than any other county (subject to the exceptions already noted), or to contemplate playing some home matches away from The Oval, and/or to double up some of their fixtures as they had done in 1909.

This time there seems to have been no discussion on these options. Instead, the decision was taken to give up fixtures, both home and away, with Derbyshire and Somerset (who, by coincidence or not, had both finished in the bottom three of the Championship table in 1911).[27] And all fixtures against the Universities were also dropped, thus breaking a tradition of playing one or other University – and often both – in each season going back to 1859.[28]

And so the chance of repeating either of the 1909 ventures was finally lost, for better or for worse. Probably for better, to judge from the reaction to the 1909 'experiment'.

Surrey away from The Oval after 1909

Reigate Priory CC hosted four more first-class fixtures between 1924 and 1936, but none were Surrey fixtures.[29] It was not until 1938 – another Australian tour year – that Surrey once again decided that first-class cricket should be taken to an out-ground in the county. This time the favour fell on the Woodbridge Road ground at Guildford, as it did also in the following year.

After the Second World War, both Guildford and Kingston – historic county town and administrative HQ of Surrey respectively – pressed Surrey CCC to incorporate a 'county week' at their venues into their fixture list. The

---

27   Surrey never again achieved a 'full set' of county fixtures until the days of the two-division Championship. They and Lancashire had both done so in 1910 and 1911, but the next instance by any county was not until 1923, by Yorkshire. Since then, full sets in the single-division Championship have been achieved only by Yorkshire and Lancashire in 1925 and 1926, by Notts in 1928, by Sussex in 1933 and 1935, by Sussex and Lancashire in 1937, and by eight counties in each year from 1960 to 1962: Glamorgan, Hampshire, Lancashire, Somerset, Sussex, Warwickshire, Worcestershire and Yorkshire.

28   The break in matches between Surrey and the Universities did not last long: Surrey played matches against one or both Universities in each season from 1919 until 1973 inclusive. Subsequently, fixtures between Surrey and the Universities have continued on an irregular basis only.

29   All four matches featured a team brought together by H.D.G.Leveson Gower, who played the touring South Africans in 1924, and Oxford University in 1934, 1935 and 1936.

county club's full Committee decided, however, that only one 'week' should be played away from The Oval in any one season, and on 4 July 1946 it was resolved that "Guildford could count on a Cricket Week in each of the next three seasons". In practice both venues hosted two Surrey first-class matches in 1946, though those at Kingston were not Championship matches.[30]   Thereafter, Kingston never again hosted a Surrey fixture, though Guildford's Cricket Week continues to this day. Since 1938 the county has played at least one first-class fixture, and latterly also at least one limited-overs match, at Woodbridge Road in every season, apart from 1964 to 1966 inclusive.[31] Surrey also ventured to Banstead for one first-class match in 1984 (against Cambridge University), and played one first-class match at Whitgift School in Croydon in each year from 2003 to 2011.

Reigate's 100-year absence from Surrey's first-class fixture list is perhaps disappointing, but not especially surprising. Reigate/Redhill is no longer the largest town in the county outside the metropolitan area (in 2011 it was fourth behind Epsom/Ewell, Guildford and Woking), and although the Priory club has been highly successful in league cricket in recent years[32], the town is not in an area where a first-class match can expect to draw a larger attendance, on a regular basis, than Guildford or Croydon. Perhaps the club missed a trick after the Second World War in not putting themselves forward for further county fixtures, as Guildford and Kingston did; but it was not really in a position to do so, as the ground had suffered bomb damage during the Blitz. With financial considerations inevitably uppermost in counties' minds, its chances of hosting another Surrey first-class match have surely now disappeared for ever.

The players after 1909

The Surrey side that played Lancashire at The Oval in June 1909 was relatively young, but it contained several of the great names of the game. Only three of the XI – Leveson Gower, Hayes and Lees – had made their first-class debuts before 1902, and all but three – Marshal, Davis and Lees – played on into the 1920s; indeed, three (Hobbs, Ducat and Leveson Gower) did not play their last first-class matches until the 1930s. Seven of the eleven - all but Marshal, Harrison, Davis and Rushby - were, or went on to be, Test cricketers. The Oval XI averaged over 360 first-class matches each over their entire careers, the range being from Davis with 113 to Hobbs with 834. The Lancashire match at The Oval was not the making

---

30   The two Kingston fixtures in 1946 were a non-Championship match against Hampshire and a match against the Combined Services. Thereafter Kingston hosted an end-of-season festival until 1953, with matches usually between 'regional' teams (North v South, or East v West) and between an England XI and a Commonwealth XI, but no Surrey county fixtures. As a curiosity, it may be noted that although Surrey played Hampshire twice at home in first-class matches in 1946, neither game was at The Oval – as well as the friendly at Kingston, the Championship match between them was played at Guildford.

31   Another curiosity: there were two first-class fixtures at Guildford in 1979, one being Surrey's Championship match against Worcestershire, and the other being a match between Oxford University and the touring Sri Lankans. Apart from the University Match at Lord's, this is one of only two first-class fixtures ever played by Oxford on a neutral ground, the other being a match against the South African Universities at Roehampton in 1967.

32   The First XI won the Surrey Premier Division title in 2005, 2007, 2008 and 2010, and the Second XI won their Divisional Championship in 2001, 2004 and 2005. In the latter year the club completed a clean sweep when the Third XI won their Divisional Championship too.

or breaking of any of its players, but the Surrey side from that game was definitely on the up: although they eventually slipped to fifth position in the Championship table in 1909, they were back up to second in 1910, and champions in 1914.

For the Surrey side at Reigate, the story was rather different. Apart from Shuter, whose 306th and last match this was, only four of the eleven at Reigate made as many as 80 first-class appearances in their entire careers (Hitch 350, Bird 192, Abel 171, Goatly 126; next came Raphael with 77). And despite repeated ructions in 1909 between the Surrey Committee and its senior professionals, which led to the departure of Jack Crawford from the club early in July and the unrelated short-term suspensions of three other players, only four of the team from Reigate - Bird, Goatly, Hitch and Platt - made it into Surrey's true First XI before the 1909 season was out, and only one of these four was anything like a regular selection for the Championship side.

Overall the Surrey side at Reigate must be seen for what it was: a makeshift combination of aspiring hopefuls who mostly didn't make it, and of former players who, apart from Shuter, never had really made it. The subsequent careers of the Reigate players, in and out of cricket, may be summarised as follows.

For **William Abel**, the Reigate match was the start of a lengthy but patchy first-class career. In all, he made 171 first-class appearances for Surrey over the years to 1926, though especially before the War he was very much in and out of Championship side. He did not play again in 1909, and only in 1910, 1912, 1914, 1919 and 1921-24 did he play as many as ten first-class matches in the season (though he managed 27 in 1922 and 25 in 1923). He never scored more than 851 runs, or took more than 37 wickets, in a single season. He died aged only 46 in 1934.

Harry Altham also did not play again for Surrey in 1909, but he reappeared for the county once in 1910, and in half a dozen Championship matches in 1912; he also finally secured an Oxford Blue in 1911, and another in 1912. After the war he made a couple of dozen appearances for Hampshire, the last in 1923. His final first-class appearance came in 1931, making him the last of the Surrey side at Reigate to appear in a first-class match. Long-serving cricket coach at Winchester, he became better known as an administrator than as a player. He held various MCC offices over the years, culminating in the Presidency in 1959/60, and was also President of Hampshire CCC from 1946 until his death in 1965. He was a leading light in schools' and youth cricket for many years, and was the author of *A History of Cricket* (first edition 1926) and of the *MCC Cricket Coaching Book* (1952). The award of the CBE in 1957 added to the DSO and MC that he had won during the First World War. With such a distinguished record, it is not surprising that he has entries in both *Who's Who* and the *Dictionary of National Biography*, a distinction shared by none of his Reigate colleagues.

For **Morice Bird**, the Reigate game could be seen as an early stepping stone towards greater things. Following the unhappy departure of Jack Crawford from Surrey early in July 1909, Bird took over the county captaincy for the games in which Leveson Gower could not, or chose not to, play. He proved to be the most regular 1909 first-teamer from among those who played at Reigate, making 11 appearances for Surrey in that year, nine of them as captain. His on-field performances in the later part of the 1909 season were modest (532 runs at 28, with no centuries), but he had done enough to secure - perhaps with a little help from his friends - a place on the tour to South Africa the following winter. There, under Leveson Gower's captaincy, he played in all five Tests – though again without setting the world alight. He also played in all five Tests in South Africa in 1913/14, and was the appointed Surrey captain in 1911, 1912 and 1913.

The unlucky **Harry Budgen** played no further first-class cricket after the game at Reigate. Born in Reigate, he also died locally, passing away at the Earlswood Asylum at Redhill in March 1944.

Edward Goatly was the only member of Surrey's Reigate XI to gain an immediate recall to the Championship side, but he could not establish himself permanently in the side, playing in only nine of Surrey's remaining 18 first-class games during the season. He continued his county career until 1914 without ever emerging as a true front-line player. He was the senior Pavilion Attendant at The Oval for several years from 1929 onwards.

Bill Hitch did not get straight back into the Championship side after the game at Reigate, but did so five matches later, and played in seven of the remaining 14 fixtures from that point. He gained a regular place in the First XI from 1910, and remained a popular Surrey stalwart until his retirement in 1925. He played in seven Tests between 1911/12 and 1921, and also umpired four Tests – three in India in 1933/34, and one at home in 1935. He was the longest survivor of Surrey's Reigate XI: he died in July 1965 when two months past his 79th birthday.

George Platt made his way into Surrey's Championship for five matches in the later part of the 1909 season, and appeared occasionally in the XI until 1914. He was head groundsman at Worcester for many years until his retirement in 1952.

John Raphael never played again for Surrey, but played occasional first-class matches for amateur XIs until 1913. He was wounded at Messines Ridge on 7 June 1917 and succumbed to his wounds at the Casualty Clearing Station at Remy Sidings four days later. As he had been born in Brussels, he has the unlikely distinction of being the only first-class cricketer who both was born and died in Belgium.

Although he too never played again for Surrey, **William Sarel** went on to have brief careers with Kent (1912-14) and Sussex (1919-21), scoring a century (against Oxford University at Hove) in his first match for Sussex. Record-books of my youth were keen to point out that he had no qualification for Sussex when he did so – evidently this was a big deal back then! He later achieved distinction as an outstanding golf club secretary, first at Beaconsfield and later at The Berkshire club.

John Shuter died in harness as Surrey's Secretary in 1920. He was taken ill after returning home from his duties at The Oval on 2 July, and died three days later at the age of 65. The game at Reigate was, unsurprisingly, his last first-class appearance, and at 54 years and 134 days old on the final day, he is still the oldest player ever to appear for Surrey in a first-class match.

Finally, **Herbert Vigar** continued as Strudwick's understudy, playing occasional first-team games in that capacity until he left the county, and first-class cricket, after the 1911 season. Like Budgen, he died at the Earlswood Asylum, in his home town of Redhill.

As for Oxford University , eight of the Reigate XI - all except Barley, Turner and Sale - went on to play in the Varsity Match at Lord's a fortnight later, in which a delayed declaration left Cambridge an impossible target before rain brought the game to an early conclusion as a draw. The first two were destined never to win a cricket Blue, though Sale did so in 1910. In the match at Lord's Evans made 79 and 46, and Salter made 53 in the first innings, while Gilbert took 6-52 in Cambridge's first innings; but otherwise there were no particular heroics from the 'Heroes of Reigate'. Perhaps Surrey allowed them to peak too soon.

What became of their team from Reigate? Well, ...

AJ Evans wrote a best-selling book *The Escaping Club* about his escape from a German PoW camp during the First World War. He played a few games for Kent in the 1920s, and appeared in a single Test for England against Australia in 1921, in which, unhappily, the common consent is that he was out of his depth.

Following his 53* at Reigate in his maiden first-class innings, **Philip le Couteur** scored 57 in his next innings (against Sussex at Hove), and thus aggregated 110 runs before being dismissed for the first time in his first-class career. His real moment of glory came in the 1910 University Match when he scored 160 and took 6-20 and 5-46 in Oxford's overwhelming victory. He later returned to his native Australia, where he made three unremarkable appearances for Victoria before settling for the academic life at the University of Western Australia.

Arnold Seitz also returned to Victoria, for whom he played 15 matches between 1910/11 and 1912/13, scoring two centuries (in separate matches) against South Australia in 1911/12. He was President of the Victoria Cricket Association from 1947 until his death in 1963, but his greatest achievements were in the field of education. He rose to become the Director of Education for Victoria from 1936 until 1948, and the following year he was made a Companion of the Order of St Michael and St George (CMG).[33]

Of the other Oxford players, **Malcolm Salter, Charles Hooman, Chris Hurst, Richard Sale** and **Humphrey Gilbert** all had relatively brief county careers (Gilbert's 72 appearances for Worcestershire being comfortably the

---

33   To prove that there is nothing new under the sun: "Above all, he has the essential quality of a first-class batsman: resource. A right-handed bat, he sometimes astounds slow leg-break bowlers bowling leg theory by making a right-about-turn when the ball is in the air, and executing a left-handed leg shot to the off side, where there are no fielders." Not a recent description of Kevin Pietersen, but a description of the batting style of Arnold Seitz from *Cricket*, 25 November 1911.

The Oxford University side that drew with Cambridge at Lord's in 1909 included eight of their team from Reigate. Back row, l to r: C.V.L.Hooman, A.J.Evans, R.O.Lagden, M.G.Salter; seated: R.L.Robinson, J.C.M.Lowe, C.S.Hurst, H.A.Gilbert, A.G.Pawson; front: P.R.le Couteur, J.A.Seitz. (Courtesy of The Bodleian Libraries, University of Oxford: shelfmark 384 c.8/1, opp page 184).

longest; he was the only one of the Oxford XI to make over 100 first-class appearances in total), while **Jack Barley, Ronald Lagden** and **Frederick Turner** played no more first-class cricket after leaving University – indeed, for Barley the Reigate fixture was his last first-class match, and for Turner 1909 was his only season of first-class cricket. Lagden became one of a small number of players to end his first-class career with a Highest Score of 99*, which he achieved for Oxford University against H.D.G.Leveson Gower's XI at Eastbourne in 1912.

Two members of the Oxford side won greater renown in other sporting fields. Frederick 'Tanky' Turner won 15 rugby union caps for Scotland between 1911 and 1914, while Charles Hooman achieved fame as an amateur golfer, playing in the Walker Cup matches against the United States in 1922 and 1923. In 1922 he won his singles match, but lost in the foursomes to an American pair that included Bobby Jones. In 1923 he played in the foursomes only, and lost.

The last survivor of the Reigate match was its top scorer Malcolm Salter, who died in June 1973 at the age of 86.

And lest we forget: If evidence were needed of the toll taken by the First World War, consider that no fewer than five of the 44 players involved in Surrey's two simultaneous fixtures in 1909 lost their lives during that conflict: Raphael, Lagden and Turner from the Reigate fixture, and Alan Marshal and Alfred Hartley from The Oval.

SURREY v LANCASHIRE

Played at Kennington Oval, Kennington, June 21, 22, 1909.

Lancashire won by an innings and 35 runs.   (Points: Surrey -1, Lancashire 1)

LANCASHIRE

1	A.Hartley	c and b Hayes	28
2	J.W.H.Makepeace	st Strudwick b Marshal	29
3	J.T.Tyldesley	b Marshal	3
4	J.Sharp	c and b Marshal	157
5	G.E.Tyldesley	c Strudwick b Hayes	1
6	A.C.MacLaren	b Hayes	2
7	*A.H.Hornby	st Strudwick b Marshal	38
8	W.Huddleston	b Hayes	15
9	H.Dean	c Strudwick b Rushby	17
10	W.Brearley	c Hobbs b Hayes	26
11	†B.Blomley	not out	1
	Extras	b 13, lb 5, w 2, nb 6	26
			343

FoW (1): 1-61, 2-64, 3-67, 4-68, 5-101, 6-225, 7-258, 8-310, 9-337, 10-343

SURREY

1	*H.D.G.Leveson-Gower	retired hurt	2	absent hurt		0
2	†H.Strudwick	b Brearley	18	(8) not out		5
3	J.B.Hobbs	b Dean	41	(2) b Brearley		13
4	E.G.Hayes	c Huddleston b Dean	25	(3) c MacLaren b Brearley		27
5	A.Marshal	b Dean	0	(6) c Sharp b Dean		14
6	J.N.Crawford	c Dean b Brearley	36	(5) c Sharp b Brearley		12
7	H.S.Harrison	b Brearley	0	(1) run out		17
8	W.E.Davis	c Blomley b Dean	0	(7) c J.T.Tyldesley b Brearley		5
9	A.Ducat	b Brearley	19	(4) c J.T.Tyldesley b Brearley		31
10	W.S.Lees	retired hurt	0	absent hurt		0
11	T.Rushby	not out	8	(9) b Dean		10
	Extras	b 10	10	b 5, lb 8, nb 2		15
			159			149

FoW (1): 1-42, 2-77, 3-77, 4-126, 5-128, 6-128, 7-128, 8-159
FoW (2): 1-23, 2-65, 3-83, 4-99, 5-115, 6-131, 7-137, 8-149

Surrey Bowling

	O	M	R	W	
Lees	25	3	79	0	
Rushby	20	4	55	1	1w,6nb
Marshal	19	4	56	4	1w
Hayes	29.4	4	94	5	
Crawford	6	0	25	0	
Harrison	3	1	8	0	

Lancashire Bowling

	O	M	R	W		O	M	R	W	
Brearley	21.2	3	79	4		24	3	77	5	2nb
Huddleston	7	2	20	0	(3)	7	0	17	0	
Dean	20	5	50	4	(2)	16.5	4	40	2	

Umpires: C.E.Dench and W.Richards.   Toss: Lancashire

Close of Play: 1st day: Surrey (1) 4-0 (Leveson-Gower 2*, Strudwick 0*).

The match was scheduled for three days but completed in two. J.Sharp's 157 took 195 minutes and included 14 fours. H.D.G.Leveson-Gower retired hurt in the Surrey first innings having scored 2 (team score 2-0). W.S.Lees retired hurt in the Surrey first innings having scored 0 (team had lost 7 wickets).

SURREY v OXFORD UNIVERSITY

Played at Park Lane, Reigate, June 21, 22, 23, 1909.

Oxford University won by an innings and 98 runs.

OXFORD UNIVERSITY

1	M.G.Salter	c Hitch b Bird	152
2	A.J.Evans	b Platt	47
3	J.A.Seitz	c Hitch b Budgen	120
4	C.V.L.Hooman	c Raphael b Budgen	117
5	*C.S.Hurst	b Abel	33
6	R.Sale	c Vigar b Abel	21
7	R.O.Lagden	c Vigar b Abel	0
8	P.R.leCouteur	not out	53
9	F.H.Turner	b Bird	2
10	H.A.Gilbert	c Hitch b Budgen	11
11	†J.C.Barley	c and b Bird	8
	Extras	b 5, lb 3, w 1, nb 4	13
			577

FoW (1): 1-154 (2), 2-286 (1), 3-364 (3), 4-417 (5), 5-447 (6), 6-453 (7), 7-538 (4), 8-541 (9), 9-556 (10), 10-577 (11)

SURREY

1	M.C.Bird	c Evans b Gilbert	11	(3) b Gilbert		4
2	W.J.Abel	c Hooman b Gilbert	4	(7) c Seitz b Evans		4
3	W.G.M.Sarel	c Evans b Lagden	57	(4) c Evans b Lagden		0
4	E.G.Goatly	c Hooman b Gilbert	6	(9) c Barley b Gilbert		69
5	H.S.Altham	run out	7	(6) b le Couteur		36
6	J.E.Raphael	b Evans	31	(5) c Turner b Evans		36
7	†H.E.Vigar	c Evans b Lagden	14	(10) not out		33
8	H.Budgen	c Hurst b le Couteur	25	c Evans b Lagden		30
9	*J.Shuter	b Turner	18	(1) b Gilbert		1
10	J.W.Hitch	c Salter b Turner	4	(11) c Turner b le Couteur		59
11	G.J.W.Platt	not out	5	(2) c Hurst b Lagden		5
	Extras	b 8, lb 1	9	b 9, lb 1, nb 1		11
			191			288

FoW (1): 1-11 (2), 2-46 (1), 3-54 (4), 4-61 (5), 5-124 (6), 6-134 (3), 7-143 (7), 8-168 (9), 9-178 (10), 10-191 (8)
FoW (2): 1-2 (1), 2-10 (2), 3-10 (4), 4-10 (3), 5-71 (5), 6-88 (6), 7-91 (7), 8-164 (8), 9-211 (9), 10-288 (11)

Surrey Bowling

	O	M	R	W	
Budgen	27	5	112	3	
Platt	39	9	88	1	4nb
Sarel	7	1	26	0	
Hitch	29	3	131	0	1w
Abel	23	7	110	3	
Goatly	3	0	21	0	
Bird	17	2	76	3	

Oxford University Bowling

	O	M	R	W		O	M	R	W	
Gilbert	16	6	25	3		27	6	77	3	
Turner	13	2	57	2	(5)	6	0	18	0	1nb
le Couteur	11.2	2	40	1		12	2	60	2	
Evans	12	3	36	1		15	5	51	2	
Lagden	11	4	24	2	(2)	22	4	71	3	

Umpires: H.Baldwin and J.Blake.   Toss: Oxford University

Close of Play: 1st day: Oxford University (1) 465-6 (Hooman 73*, le Couteur 8*); 2nd day: Surrey (2) 151-7 (Goatly 36*, Budgen 30*).
M.G.Salter's 152 took 220 minutes and included 18 fours. J.A.Seitz's 120 took 140 minutes and included 21 fours.
C.V.L.Hooman's 117 took 150 minutes and included 17 fours and 2 fives.

2: Warwickshire in 1919

Derbyshire v Warwickshire (Derby) and
Warwickshire v Worcestershire (Edgbaston), August 1919

WHY AND WHO

Background

In both its inception and its execution, the cricket season of 1919 was unusual.

Following the Armistice in November 1918, moves were rapidly made to arrange something approaching a normal season for the following summer. But there were stirrings for change. At a meeting of the Advisory County Cricket Committee (ACCC) on 16 December 1918, the counties resolved (though only by ten votes to five) to reintroduce the County Championship in 1919, and at the same time to limit county matches to two days. This decision was not universally supported. By the following February *The Times* was contending that it had brought about a "crisis in the cricket world", and opined that the decisions made in December were made in haste, and would be repented at leisure: "It is scarcely an exaggeration to suggest that the many questions involved in so revolutionary a change as two-day county matches had not been considered with sufficient care ... [they] were not considered judgments, but were ill-digested and not thought out".

The Times argued that the proposed changes would lead to declining revenues but rising expenditure for the counties, and it concluded that the best approach would be to "abolish the Championship for 1919 ... [to] allow the counties to play [each other in friendlies over] two or three days, as they desired[.] You would then be able to compare the two systems side by side, in the same season, which would be an excellent guide for the future".[34]

But despite *The Times*'s thundering, a further ACCC meeting on 5 February 1919 confirmed "by a large majority" the decisions to proceed with the two-day County Championship in 1919, although earlier proposals to dispense with the tea interval and to ban Saturday starts were relaxed.

The way was now clear for the county secretaries to draw up a fixture list for the coming season, which they did on 6 February. However, their list was to a degree provisional, not least because of uncertainties regarding whether or not a suggested tour by an Australian Services team would go ahead. The fixtures printed in *The Times* on 7 February included some for the Australian Services side, but also some alternative fixtures in the event that the tour did not go ahead. On the same day *The Times* reported that a decision about the tour had been postponed for a month. The fixture list published a little later in *Wisden* is slightly different from that in *The Times*, and is prefaced by the remarks "The proposed tour of the

---

34   The quotations in this and the preceding paragraph are all from an unsigned article in *The Times* on 5 February 1919. However it seems highly likely that it was written by Pelham Warner, as some of its content is very similar to that of a letter of his that was printed in *The Times* on 28 January 1919, and moreover the writer on 5 February appeared privy to the changing views of Middlesex on the matter: Middlesex was, of course, Warner's county.

Australian Services Team having been cancelled, additional County and other matches will no doubt be arranged. It is also likely that some dates will be altered to admit of more Saturday starts".[35]

The point of this background is to show the haste and uncertainties that surrounded the drawing up of fixtures for the 1919 season, and by extension the relative ill-preparedness of cricket to return to something like its pre-war structure. The position as seen at the start of the season was well summed up in the Notes by the Editor in *Wisden*, when he wrote that "County cricket in 1919, after a blank of four seasons, [is] bound to be a very speculative and experimental business".

Individual counties were in some confusion too. For several, the War or the war years had taken away some of their established or promising players, while the lack of cricket over the war years had done nothing to improve many counties' finances.

Among the worst hit were Warwickshire, who had lost the highly promising Percy Jeeves to the War, Frank Foster to injury, and Sep Kinneir and Sydney Santall to anno domini. For the 1919 season they were left with only five players from the regular 1914 side – and three of those were aged 44 or older.

Worcestershire too had suffered particularly badly. They had not lost so many 'big name' players, although R.E.Foster had died at the age of only 36 early in 1914, and the promising Frank Chester would be unable to play again following the loss of an arm in the War. But they had lost too much financially for their future to be secure. In 1917 the retiring Chairman of the club suggested to his successor that it should be wound up[36], but the subsequent generosity of members and supporters had provided enough to keep it afloat – just.

Nevertheless, after the War, with a new season of county cricket just around the corner, the Worcestershire Committee felt it necessary to convene a special meeting "to consider what steps should be taken to run an eleven for the coming season". The meeting was held at the Star Hotel, Worcester, on 4 January 1919. The Chairman, Judge Richard Amphlett, reported that the club's reserve – a sum of £500 – was comparatively small, and put forward the view that they "could not indulge in first-class cricket on the old lines". Instead, "he thought they might develop such cricket talent as would bring them in due course into line with some of the first-class counties again". The club captain, Major W.H.Taylor, confirmed the view that they could not run a first-class county team on the old lines, and said that "he preferred to run an amateur team with one or two professionals when available". He also thought that "there would be no difficulty in getting fixtures with six county teams [which turned out to be

---

35   The Services tour was indeed cancelled, because of the difficulty of getting a representative team together. In due course a very similar programme, but omitting three proposed 'Test matches', was arranged for an Australian Imperial Forces (AIF) side.

36   "When Lord Cobham persuaded [me] to succeed him as Chairman of the Committee Lord Cobham suggested that [I] should takes the steps necessary to inter the club, and that the best memorial would be the payment of 20s in the £". Speech by Richard Amphlett at Worcestershire CCC meeting on 4 January 1919, as reported in the *Worcestershire Chronicle* 11 January 1919.

the minimum number required to compete in the Championship in 1919]", but "the first thing they had to find out was what players were available".

At the end of the meeting, Major Taylor's proposals were carried unanimously; and by so doing Worcestershire took the decision to withdraw from the County Championship for 1919.[37]

So it was that the fixture list agreed (provisionally, and on an incomplete basis) at the county secretaries' meeting on 6 February 1919 did not include any Worcestershire matches. Neither did the slightly different fixture list subsequently published in *Wisden*. If Worcestershire were going to play any county matches, they would have to fit their fixtures around the Championship dates of other counties.

Except that it wasn't quite as simple as that.

Complications, and resolution
In every year between 1900 (the year after Worcestershire joined the County Championship) and 1914, Warwickshire and Worcestershire had met in a Championship match over the August Bank Holiday, which at this time was on the first Monday in August. This was one of a series of 'traditional' Bank Holiday fixtures, usually between neighbours: Yorkshire v Lancashire, Gloucestershire v Somerset, Northants v Leicestershire; sometimes between counties with no special geographical links – Derbyshire v Essex, Surrey v Notts; and also between Kent, Sussex, Hampshire and Middlesex, in pairings which varied from year to year.

When county cricket was being mooted for 1919, Warwickshire were quickly off the mark in seeking to resume their Bank Holiday rivalry with Worcestershire. Although the primary source records have not survived, we know that this was so because of a reference in reports of the Worcestershire CCC meeting on 4 January 1919:
> "Mr [W.G.] Spreckley asked if county teams would accept matches with Worcestershire, and Major Taylor said Warwickshire had already offered them Bank Holiday dates. He had no doubt that Somerset and Gloucester would [also] play them."[38]

So a fixture between Warwickshire and Worcestershire over the August Bank Holiday (which was on Monday August 4th in 1919) was already pencilled in, if not confirmed (we unfortunately can't say for certain which), in advance of the county secretaries' meeting on 6 February which produced the first 'official' fixture list for the season. No doubt the August fixture was proposed for Edgbaston, as Warwickshire had hosted all the August Bank Holiday fixtures between the counties since 1909, and all but three of these fixtures since they were inaugurated in 1900.

---

37   The details of the 4 January meeting are taken from the report in the *Worcestershire Chronicle* of 11 January 1919. There is no express reference in that report to Worcestershire withdrawing from the County Championship, but that was the clear consequence of the views expressed and decisions taken at the meeting.

38   *Worcestershire Chronicle* 11 January 1919. In the event, and despite the expectation at the 4 January meeting that Worcestershire would be able to get fixtures with six other counties, these three were the only counties to play Worcestershire in 1919.

But Bank Holiday matches were potentially among the most lucrative games for all counties. There were 15 counties in the Championship in 1919, all of whom would want an August Bank Holiday fixture. In theory this meant that there was one county left over, unable to play a Championship match over the Bank Holiday, but this was not a problem as it left a space for the fifteenth county to play the touring AIF.

There was thus no realistic scope for any one county to opt out of playing a Championship or tourist fixture over the Bank Holiday in order that they could play someone else, however lucrative or 'traditional' that alternative fixture might have been. To have done so would have left another county in the lurch and fixtureless on these important dates. We don't know whether Warwickshire, having already arranged the Bank Holiday fixture with Worcestershire, raised any objection at the county secretaries' meeting on 6 February to being obliged to play a Championship match on the same dates.[39] But the upshot was that at that meeting they were slated to play Derbyshire at Derby over the Bank Holiday – thus incidentally starting a tradition of August Bank Holiday matches between these two teams which lasted until 1958, apart from the two seasons of 1936 and 1937 when they reverted to the even-more-traditional Bank Holiday match against Worcestershire.[40]

So Warwickshire were now more or less committed to playing both Derbyshire and Worcestershire over the August Bank Holiday of 1919. Whether they subsequently tried to rearrange either fixture to avoid the clash we don't know: I have not found any references in the local newspapers to any moves towards such a rearrangement, but that is not conclusive proof that there were none. There was certainly enough slack in the fixture list agreed on 6 February to have allowed the Worcestershire match to be rearranged so that it did not clash with one of Warwickshire's Championship fixtures, but for whatever reason this did not happen. Perhaps Warwickshire and Worcestershire were content with the double-header arrangement: no doubt the prospect of a good Bank Holiday crowd at Edgbaston for a match between neighbours appealed to Warwickshire (remembering that they were accustomed to a home fixture over the holiday, so playing a probably-less-lucrative Championship match at Derby broke with this pattern). No doubt too there was a general wish to resume the traditional rivalries between the counties in as close to pre-war circumstances as was possible.

Thus it came about that Warwickshire were booked for a double-header on Monday and Tuesday 4-5 August 1919 (like Championship matches in

39   The minutes of the 6 February meeting – at which Worcestershire were not represented – indicate that the Secretaries indulged in a lengthy discussion about the effects on the game of the newly-introduced Entertainment Tax, but say nothing at all about the nitty-gritty of the drawing-up of the fixture list.

40   For most counties, the post-war fixture lists maintained the pre-war 'traditional' August Bank Holiday fixtures. But the customary pre-war Bank Holiday fixture between Derbyshire and Essex was scrapped, which is how Derbyshire came to be available to play Warwickshire from 1919 onwards. Essex were paired with Kent for 1919, but from 1920 onwards they began a tradition of playing Worcestershire – newly freed from their traditional fixture with Warwickshire – over the holiday. If Worcestershire had stayed in the Championship in 1919 it seems likely that their Bank Holiday fixture with Warwickshire would have been able to continue throughout the post-war years and beyond, leaving Derbyshire presumably back with Essex.

1919, all Worcestershire's inter-county matches that year were two-day affairs). Unlike the Surrey instance in 1909, there seems to be no extant start-of-season fixture list which shows *both* games on those dates. But as already noted, none of Worcestershire's fixtures were included in any such fixture lists.[41] I have also traced no other early-season statement or comment acknowledging that Warwickshire were due to play two county matches simultaneously during the season.

So we must just settle for the fact that the two matches have been arranged for the same dates. Let's note too that the 'more important' match, Warwickshire's Championship match with Derbyshire, was arranged after their match with Worcestershire had been fixed for the same dates, and thus in the knowledge that a clash, or a double-header, would result. Perhaps if the Edgbaston match with Worcestershire had not been mooted until after the initial Championship list had been drawn up, it would not have been fixed for the Bank Holiday, tradition notwithstanding. In which case – no story. But happily for lovers of the arcane, that was not the case.

Players: Warwickshire

Despite the difficulties resulting from the War, Warwickshire were able to appoint nine professionals to the groundstaff for 1919, six of whom had played for the county pre-war.[42] But recognising the weakness of their post-war squad, Warwickshire undertook a search for new talent throughout the season:

> "The County is being systematically scoured for players of ability, and no promising player in a public school, or a local or village club, is being denied the opportunity of being tested at the nets, or given a trial in a minor match to see what he is made of."[43]

For their first Championship match since August 1914, against Surrey at The Oval on Friday 6 June 1919, Warwickshire fielded a side that featured eight of their retained professionals – all but Ernest Suckling - together with the amateurs Jack Parsons Commander Charles Cowan, and Willie Hands, who captained the side in the absence of the official captain George Stephens. This XI included five of those who had played in Warwickshire's last pre-war match, while the other six had for the most part at least some first-class experience. Only one (Harry Austin) was making his first-class debut, while one other (Verner Luckin) was making his debut for

---

41   We know that the Warwickshire fixture was effectively in place by 4 January 1919, and – from a brief item in *The Times* on 1 February 1919, reporting Gloucestershire's acceptance of fixtures with Worcestershire - we know that the fixtures between those two counties were arranged at about the same time as the main county fixture list was being drawn up. Thus Worcestershire's fixtures with Warwickshire and Gloucestershire, at least, *could* have been included in the fixture list published following the county secretaries' meeting on 6 February, and/or in the list subsequently published in *Wisden*; but they were not.

42   The *Birmingham Post* on 26 April 1919 reported that eight professionals had been appointed. The five 'old hands' listed were W.G.Quaife, C.S.Baker, C.Charlesworth, L.T.A.Bates and H.Howell; the newcomers were V.V.Luckin (who had previously played for Hampshire), H.Austin and E.Suckling. The omission of E.J.Smith from the paper's list of retained professionals is surprising, and may be simply an error on the newspaper's part. I have assumed that he was included on the county's staff right from the start of the season – he certainly played in the very first match.

43   *Birmingham Mail*, 31 July 1919

Warwickshire, having previously played elsewhere.

The season did not start well for the weakened Warwickshire side. By early August they had not won any of their ten matches, and they were stuck on the bottom of the Championship table as the only county without a victory. They had yet to find anything approaching a settled side. 23 different players had appeared in the ten matches, and although nine had appeared in seven or more matches (Willie Quaife was the only one to have appeared in all ten), as many as six had made just a single appearance, and four others had played in only two or three matches. Five of the 23 were first-class debutants, another two had made their debuts earlier in 1919 for one or other of the Universities, and three more had made their Warwickshire debuts after playing elsewhere before the War.

So when at the end of July Warwickshire had to pick two sides to play over the August Bank Holiday, the selection of neither side was straightforward. As with Surrey in 1909, the selectors understandably gave priority to the side to play in the Championship fixture at Derby. But even for this game they made four changes from the side in the previous Championship match at Old Trafford, giving a county debut to Freddie Calthorpe (who was to become the county captain in 1920) and recalling Cowan, Mick Waddy and Gerry Rotherham (all of whom had appeared in the county side earlier in the season), at the expense of A.F. 'Spinney' Lane, John Stevenson (whose appearance at Old Trafford turned out to be his one and only first-class match), William Harris, and Luckin. The selected team, with their number of appearances for Warwickshire in their ten matches to date, was as follows:

L.T.A.Bates (9), E.J.Smith (9), W.G.Quaife (10), R.L.Holdsworth (3), E.F.Waddy (3), F.S.G.Calthorpe (0), G.A.Rotherham (2), Commander C.F.R.Cowan (1), G.W.Stephens (captain; 7), W.C.Hands (5), and H.Howell (9).

In theory enough other players had already played for Warwickshire in 1919 to make up another eleven to play the Bank Holiday match with Worcestershire. But not all were available, or were considered for selection. Crowther Charlesworth and Jack Parsons, both of whom would surely have played at Derby if fit or available, were missing through illness and military duties respectively; Frank Field was only intermittently available during 1919, and John Stevenson was also not available; while Harry Austin, Charlie Baker and Eric Crockford had shown insufficient form in their earlier matches to justify an automatic place in the side for the Worcestershire game - particularly given Warwickshire's wish, already noted, to give opportunities to promising players from all over the county in the hope of turning up new players of ability.

That left six players who had played in Championship matches already in 1919 who were not needed at Derby, but who were otherwise available and were regarded as being in some sort of form. These were **Verner Luckin**[44], who had played in the county's first seven matches of the season, and had reappeared for the Old Trafford match; **William Harris**, who had made

---

[44]   Those selected to play in the match at Edgbaston are named in bold type in the following sections.

four appearances for the county so far in 1919 – he had the dual assets of being an amateur who could captain the side, and also a wicket-keeper; **Harold Benjamin, Alec Hastilow** and **Ernest Suckling**, each of whom had played just a single county match so far; and Spinney Lane, who had been a regular in the county XI until the end of July but then dropped out of sight for a while (he was a successful self-made industrialist, whose work prevented him playing regular county cricket; in fact he did not play another first-class match until 1921). Apart from Lane, all these players were selected for the Edgbaston match against Worcestershire, and on that basis one could say that this core of the side against Worcestershire was pretty much the best or most experienced that Warwickshire were able to assemble.

That still left six places to be filled. Warwickshire had no official Second XI in 1919, although promising players had the opportunity to bring themselves to notice in matches for, or against, the Warwickshire Club & Ground (C&G). These matches were supervised by Sydney Santall, now the county's coach, and it is believed that he played a major, if not the major, part in the selection of the side to play Worcestershire.[45]   The full team was announced on 31 July as follows; the total number of first-class matches in which they had each already played, and the number already played in 1919, are in brackets:

> W.H.Harris (captain and wicket-keeper, 11 first-class matches in all, 4 in 1919), H.Venn (0, 0), J.A.Smart (0, 0), R.H.M.Burton (0, 0), C.A.F.Hastilow (1, 1), E.P.Hewetson (0, 0), F.R.Santall (0, 0), V.V.Luckin (18, 8), H.L.Benjamin (1, 1), E.Suckling (1, 1) and A.L.Howell (0, 0).

On the same date the *Birmingham Mail* described the new selections as follows:

> "There will be included in the eleven several young cricketers who have been doing remarkably well in local games, namely R.H.M.Burton of Rugby Town; C.A.F.Hastilow of Birmingham University; E.P.Hewitson [sic] of Shrewsbury School; F.R. Santall the wonderful secondary school boy, and J.Smart of Chilvers Coton, the son of the former Wiltshire professional, who has the reputation of being a capital batsman. ... [A.L.] Howell is a younger brother of the Warwickshire fast bowler. He has been fulfilling an engagement at Uppingham School, and is reported to be a bowler of considerable promise. H.Venn is a Coventry cricketer who has been playing very well this season."

The same report also noted that "J.F.Stevenson would have played had he been able to make arrangements to do so". And so passed his chance of doubling his career total of first-class matches.

A further word is called for about some of the less familiar names in this side. I have found only limited evidence to confirm whether or not any of them were indeed "doing remarkably well in local games", but all of them came to the side with some form or reputation behind them.

Young **Reggie Santall** was already well known in local cricket circles for his exceptional feats in school and club cricket. He had scored 84 in a

---

45   As stated in an article about the Worcestershire match in *The Cricket Statistician* issue 11 (Autumn 1975), pp 19-21.

A youthful Reggie Santall.

match for Kings Heath in 1918, and performed "some remarkable feats with both the bat and the ball for the Central Secondary School" (*Birmingham Post*, 21 May 1919). In May 1919 - still only 15 years old - he had scored 61 in 35 minutes for Warwickshire C&G against a strong Moseley side, in his first-ever match at Edgbaston. In his last match of the 1919 school season, on 19 July, he had scored 111* out of 130-6 against Camp Hill, and then taken 6-20 in the Camp Hill innings. There may or may not have been an element of nepotism in his selection for the Worcestershire match[46], but he was clearly a player of great promise, and his selection could not be criticised as in any way irrational.

Two others of the final selection were emerging or established players at Warwickshire clubs who had presumably made a good impression on Sydney Santall in C&G matches earlier in 1919: 19-year-old **Reginald Burton** when scoring 55* for a combined Coventry and Rugby XI against the C&G on 25 June, and **Horace 'Harry' Venn** – who had turned out for the county Second XI before the war - when making 60 for the C&G against a combined Griff Colliery and Chilvers Coton XI on 24 July. As noted, **Albert Howell** - younger brother of Warwickshire's future Test cricketer Harry Howell - had been recommended by the county to Uppingham School at the start of the season "for engagement as a net bowler, under Humphreys (Kent)" (*Birmingham Post*, 26 April 1919); evidently the county saw some potential in him at an early stage, but felt this would be best realised through the day-to-day rigours of school coaching rather than in less frequent club or C&G games nearer home. **Jack Smart** was another whose selection seems to have been based more on promise than on actual performances: in the only C&G game in which he played of which I have traced details, against Pickwick at the end of June, he scored only 11 while his younger brother Cyril made 65 (and an otherwise unheralded bowler named Purshouse took 8-50 in a single innings, never to be heard of again).

Finally **Edward Hewetson** had only just turned 17 when selected, and still had two full years at school remaining to him. A genuinely fast bowler and aggressive batsman, he made 410 runs (topping the batting averages) and took 32 wickets for Shrewsbury School in 1919, although the only reference to him in *Wisden*'s public schools review says no more than that he "bowled fairly well on occasions".

Thus the players selected to play Worcestershire over the Bank Holiday at the start of August could all be seen as merit selections, in the context of Warwickshire's search that season for promising players who might have a future in cricket. Whether this was the very best 'second team' that could have been assembled may be open to question, but that was not the only

---

46   The same article as referred to in the previous footnote also suggests that Santall showed favouritism in selecting his son Reggie in the side, ahead of possible claims by Ted Hampton (later the Warwickshire statistician), and by the 18-year-old Bob Wyatt.

aim behind its selection. True, the side was to a degree experimental – but that was true of several county sides in this difficult 1919 season. In the circumstances in which Warwickshire found themselves this year, it was an entirely reasonable and rational selection, given that the players for the Championship match had to be excluded.

Players: Worcestershire

In accordance with the decision taken at the Star Hotel on 4 January 1919, Worcestershire announced late in April that none of the old professionals of the county team had been engaged for 1919, considering instead that "it is thought to be possible to build up an entirely new side".[47] Nevertheless, team selection for their major matches in 1919 was no easier than for their neighbours.

In the last season before the War, the county had used 25 players in their 22 Championship matches, of whom nine had played in 18 matches or more, five played between seven and ten matches, and the remaining 11 played between one and three matches, as many as seven playing only once.

Of the nine 'regulars', only six were in a position to resume cricket for the county in 1919: Ernest Bale (the wicket-keeper), Frederick Bowley, Dick Burrows, Alfred Cliff, Frederick Pearson and William Taylor. Unsurprisingly, these were not young men. The first four named were already in their 40s, with Pearson not far behind, and Taylor the junior of the group at 35. Of the other 'regulars', M.K.Foster was not available to play in 1919, John Cuffe had retired, and the very promising Frank Chester had lost an arm in the war and could not return to the first-class game as a player.

The five middle-rankers from 1914 had also suffered significant losses, with Christopher Collier killed in the War, Spinney Lane transferring his allegiances to Warwickshire, G.N.Foster out of county cricket until he returned for Kent in 1921, and Bertie Stevens having retired. 34-year-old Arthur Conway was the only one of the five still available to Worcestershire in 1919.

So with only a small number of established players available to them in 1919, and several of them ageing, the county was obliged to give chances to several inexperienced players in their first-class matches. By the end of July they had used 18 players in their five first-class matches so far, six of whom (Thomas Allchurch, Robert Berkeley, John Coventry, Edward Nesfield, Capt. Geoffrey Sheppard and Benjamin Tipper) made their first-class debuts in one or another of these games, and two others of whom (Frank Harry and Arthur Jewell) made their debuts for Worcestershire after brief pre-war careers elsewhere. The rest of their teams was made up from the seven pre-war survivors just mentioned. Bale, Cliff and Taylor had played in all five matches so far, Bowley and Conway in three, Burrows in two, and Pearson in just one.

---

47   *Worcestershire Chronicle* 26 April 1919. In the event, six of the 25 cricketers who played for the county in their nine first-class matches of 1919 were professionals, all of whom had represented the county in 1914 or earlier. As many as four professionals played together in five of the matches, and three in three of the others.

The sixth game of Worcestershire's county season was the Bank Holiday match against Warwickshire at Edgbaston. Of the 'regulars', **Ernest Bale** and **Alfred Cliff** were both selected for this game (thus maintaining their 100% appearance record for the season), along with **Arthur Conway** and **Dick Burrows**; why and how Taylor, Bowley and Pearson negotiated an opt-out is not recorded. Other prime candidates for the side at Edgbaston were surely those who had appeared in three of the five earlier matches - Coventry, Fred Hunt, Tipper and James Turner, together with the Chilean-born, South African-raised brothers Maurice and Arthur Jewell.[48] But five of this six (all but Hunt) were amateurs, who could no doubt be picky as to where they spent their Bank Holiday. In the end, of these only **Fred Hunt** and **James Turner** - the latter named as captain - found themselves on the Edgbaston team-sheet.

Six down, five places to fill. For reasons now lost - but presumably related to the earlier-stated wish to "develop such talent as would bring them in line with some of the first-class counties again" - the selectors decided to pick five men who hadn't appeared for the county at all in 1919, rather than giving a further chance to any of those who had already made their county debuts earlier in the season without achieving striking success. All five of those selected were, inevitably, amateurs. Four of them had played no previous first-class cricket, while the fifth had played just a single game at that level, six years previously.

Exactly how these five came to be chosen is a mystery. **Frederick Abbott** and **Rupert Cave-Rogers**[49] were both 17-year-olds from Malvern College, though their school records for the season - respectively, second and eighth in the batting averages, and not featuring at all in the bowling averages - did not immediately suggest that they were demanding a trial in the county side. However, both had done well in a match for the school against Herefordshire a week before the game at Edgbaston, Abbott scoring 68 and Cave-Rogers 34 (including only one single). The Herefordshire side included H.K.Foster, and I suspect that his influence weighed strongly in the final decision to include them in the XI for Edgbaston. Both also played for the county in a one-day game against Wolverhampton on the Saturday before the Edgbaston game (2 August), but with considerably less success: Cave-Rogers made 4, and Abbott a duck. This suggests that the side for Edgbaston had already been picked before the start of the Bank Holiday weekend; but sadly, local newspapers are silent on the when and how of the selection of the Worcestershire side.

Of the other amateurs, 19-year-old **Herbert Isaac** had been at Harrow School, and played in the wartime match against Eton in 1917 (with little success), but his name does not appear in the school's averages or reports in *Wisden* for this or any other year, indicating that he was never a regular in the School XI. He was the son and nephew respectively of two former

---

48   J.E.V. Jewell, who played for Surrey II in 1909 (see page 18), was another brother of this pair.

49   CricketArchive names this player as R.A.C.Rogers, saying that he adopted the surname Cave-Rogers later in his life. But he is named as Cave-Rogers in the Malvern College averages in the 1919 and 1920 editions of *Wisden*, which indicates that that was the name he used at the time of the match at Edgbaston in August 1919. He shared his exact date of birth - 27 May 1902 - with one of Warwickshire's schoolboy selections, Edward Hewetson.

Worcestershire players who were killed in the War - perhaps there was a sentimental element to his selection? **Harold Shakespeare** (his full initials are 'W.H.N.' and he is identified as 'William Shakespeare' in CricketArchive, but I am assured by those with local knowledge that he was known by his second Christian name) was Worcester born and bred, and educated at the Royal Grammar School there; but he was now 25 years old, so whatever it was that gained him selection, it wasn't his school performances. Finally, **James Higgs-Walker** had been in the Repton XI alongside the likes of Freddie Calthorpe and Miles Howell in 1912, but failed to progress beyond the Freshman's match at Oxford the following season. His sole previous first-class match, for Worcestershire against Gloucestershire at Cheltenham in August 1913, had hardly been an unmitigated triumph, with scores of 0 and 0* to go with bowling figures of 2-0-20-0; but for the Edgbaston game he had the advantage of being principally a bowler in an otherwise bowler-light side, so he joined Burrows, Conway and Hunt to make up essentially a four-man attack.

The Worcestershire side chosen for the match at Edgbaston was therefore a classic mix of callow youth and experience, with the former dominating. With their total number of previous first-class matches in brackets, along with the number already played in 1919, the selected XI was as follows:

F.J.Abbott (0, 0), E.W.Bale (142, 5), R.D.Burrows (273, 2), R.A.Cave-Rogers (0, 0), A.T.Cliff (31, 5), A.J.Conway (28, 3), J.A.Higgs-Walker (1, 0), F.Hunt (56, 3), H.W. Isaac (0, 0), W.H.N.Shakespeare (0, 0) and J.W.C.Turner (captain; 18, 5).

The Worcestershire side lines up outside the pavilion at Edgbaston. Standing, l to r: R.A.Cave-Rogers, A.Machell (scorer), F.Hunt, R.D.Burrows, A.J.Conway, E.W.Bale, H.W.Isaac; seated: A.T.Cliff, J.A.Higgs-Walker, J.W.C.Turner, W.H.N.Shakespeare, F.J.Abbott

With 549 first-class appearances between them before the Edgbaston game started, this side beat Warwickshire's pre-match aggregate by a cool 517. But aggregating the players' *eventual* total of first-class appearances, Warwickshire win by 915 to 637, suggesting that the overall balance of skill may have lain with the home side. In terms of age rather than experience Worcestershire had a clear edge, with an average age of 31y 244d (their side included four players in their 40s and three teenagers, with Dick Burrows the oldest at 48:60 and Cave-Rogers the youngest at 17:69) against Warwickshire's 24y 296d (with only one player - Harris, 35:217 - over 30 and four teenagers, the youngest being Santall, just 23 days past his 16th birthday).

On this evidence, you might have thought we were in for a reasonably close game ...

PLAY!

The descriptions of play and the quotations in this section are all derived from the Birmingham Post unless stated. Complete scorecards of the two matches are included on pages 65 and 66.

Warwickshire had had a ten-day break from first-class cricket when, on August Bank Holiday Monday 4 August 1919 their two teams began their battles with Derbyshire in the Championship at Derby, and against Worcestershire in a friendly at Edgbaston. As already mentioned, their season had not gone well so far – played ten, won none, drawn five, lost five. None of the defeats was even close: three were by an innings (including in their two most recent fixtures), and the other two were both by seven wickets. To be fair, two of the draws may be regarded as 'winning draws' – at Edgbaston on 24 June they had Surrey 90-6 in their second innings, needing 186 to win, when the end came; while the following match against Leicestershire at Hinckley ended with Warwickshire 9-0 in their second innings needing a total of 118 for victory. One of the other three draws, against Lancashire, was definitely a 'losing draw', while neither team had a clear ascendancy at the end of the other two.

Derbyshire meanwhile were having a rather better season. On the morning of 4 August they stood sixth in the Championship table with three wins from ten games. Their wins included a seven-wicket success against Warwickshire at Edgbaston early in June, where Warwickshire's first innings lead of 69 had been insufficient to avoid defeat in the face of fine pace bowling by Bill Bestwick (7-50 in Warwickshire's second innings 155, to follow 5-103 in the first innings) and determined second innings batting that made light work of a target of 225.

For Worcestershire the season was proving predictably difficult. They had begun with a commendable draw against Gloucestershire towards the end of June, a late declaration setting their visitors 150 to win in what turned out to be 21 overs; Gloucestershire had reached 109-4 when Time was called. Against Somerset a fortnight later they bowled their visitors out twice, and needed 210 in the fourth innings for victory; things looked good at 132-3, but they then collapsed and were no doubt content when time ran out with their score on 149-8, after 71 overs. They then lost by four wickets to a scratch side raised by H.K.Foster, after being bowled out for 87 in their first innings; lost by an innings and 203 to the AIF side; and lost by an innings and 96 in the return with Somerset, their innings totals being just 67 and 78.

So only Derbyshire could face the Bank Holiday fixtures with any confidence. The scene is set ...

Day 1 - Monday 4 August 1919

The forecast for both Derby and Birmingham was for typical Bank Holiday weather: cloudy or dull with some rain, and only moderate temperatures *(The Times)*. At Derby at least, the forecasters were spot on. It was not really a day for cricket there at all, but there was a Bank Holiday crowd to be entertained:

"Had it not been desirable to conciliate a Bank Holiday crowd of 4000, it is doubtful if the players would have been on the field half the time they actually spent there. With rain falling persistently, the conditions were really unfit for first-class cricket. Fielders found the wet and greasy ball difficult to hold, and catches that would have been brought off easily in normal conditions escaped the grip, while the batsmen were led into miscalculations of which they might not ordinarily have been guilty."

Nevertheless, play at Derby started on time in what were described as "ideal conditions"; it must have been a little later that the weather took a turn for the worse. Warwickshire won the toss and batted. The second ball of the match was to prove costly, Len Oliver dropping Len Bates in the slips. Oliver also missed a hard chance from Tiger Smith when he was 14, but after these early escapes the openers enjoyed themselves. They added 137 in 90 minutes before the first wicket fell when Smith was caught at point for 72, with eight fours, "relying principally on hard drives interspersed with some delightful late cuts".

Willie Quaife was out at 201, by which time "stoppages for rain [had] consumed so much time [that] less than four hours' play remained, with the possibility of further interruptions; there was, consequently, a great inducement to the rest of the side to take risks and force the pace. The policy they adopted was right spirited and commendable, even if it was not achieved with entire success in every instance".

In execution of this policy, Warwickshire went from 201-1 to 236-5 (when Bates left for 119, which included only eight fours) and 287-8, before late flurries took them to an all-out score of 359, made in 4 hours 20 minutes *(The Field)* at a commendable - especially in the conditions - run-rate of 3.72 runs per over.

For Derbyshire, the bowling honours went once again to 44-year-old Bill Bestwick, whose analysis of 44.2-4-178-8 took him to 20 wickets in three innings against Warwickshire this season. His accuracy is demonstrated by the fact that 15 of those 20 wickets were 'bowled' dismissals.

Warwickshire's innings ended at 6.15 pm *(Manchester Guardian)*, but with the long playing hours in operation in 1919, Derbyshire still had time for 55 minutes' batting before the close of play. They uncharacteristically caught the mood set by the later Warwickshire batsmen, for their runs came "with a rapidity that aroused [their] supporters to high enthusiasm", with the usually sedate Oliver in particular showing an enterprise that "had a smack of novelty". By the close at 7.30 Derbyshire had reached 75-1 with Oliver on 48*. With 434 runs and 11 wickets off something like 115-120 overs, the Bank Holiday crowd had surely had a thoroughly entertaining, if sometimes wet, day, at the end of which the honours between the two sides were even.

The same could also be said at the end of the first day's play at Edgbaston, where 478 runs were scored on the first day between Warwickshire and Worcestershire. From the limited reports of the day's play we learn that the match was watched by "a large holiday crowd" *(Evening Despatch)*, and that weather conditions were clearly better than those at Derby, as apart from a shower that prolonged the lunch interval, a full day's cricket was played.

Worcestershire won the toss and batted, and "with the exception of R.A.Cave-Rogers, the early batsmen were all seen to advantage". Warwickshire suffered an early blow with the loss from the attack of first-change bowler Albert Howell after he had bowled only three overs. Howell had begun well: his first ball "had Rogers hopelessly beaten" *(Evening Despatch)*, and thereafter "he bowled in promising style for a few overs", picking up Cave-Rogers' wicket with a caught-and-bowled in the process. But he was less fortunate with another return hit, for he split his left hand [not his bowling hand] in stopping a hard drive from either Shakespeare or Hunt, and could play no further part in the game.

What happened next gives rise to some controversy, not at the match itself but for later statisticians. The *Birmingham Post* reports that Howell "was forced to retire, and by the courtesy of the Worcester captain his place was filled by G.Tyler, son of the old Moseley captain". The question that engages the statistician's mind is whether this man - in full, George Edward Tyler - was a full substitute for Howell, entitled to bat and bowl (though in point of fact he did neither), because if he was, he is surely entitled to an entry in the list of first-class cricketers, even though he played in no other first-class match. Or was he 'just' a sub, entitled to field but nothing more?

The report in the *Post*, with its reference to the involvement of the Worcestershire captain in the decision to bring Tyler into the match, together with that paper's later coverage (of which more below) clearly points to the former. But no other contemporary or recent source expressly states that Tyler was a full substitute, and he is not listed as a first-class cricketer in the ACS *Who's Who of Cricketers*. More recently, the scorecard in the ACS's 1919 scorebook omits Tyler from the listed Warwickshire side, but includes a footnote to the effect that he "replaced" Howell, without batting or bowling: a nice bit of fence-sitting, perhaps![50]

Back to the cricket. Following Howell's departure, the *Post* tells us that Shakespeare hit in spirited fashion for Worcestershire, after a slow start, and that Burrows' hitting of in the opening stages of his innings "was

---

50   But see footnote 56 below.

marked with much of his old-time vigour". In all, Burrows' 82 took about 1¾ hours and included ten fours *(The Field)*. Apart from Cave-Rogers all the top order batsmen made useful scores, and although the full fall of wickets is not available the *Post* indicates that the sixth wicket fell with the score on 252. The last five wickets fell relatively quickly to the bowling of Santall and Smart, who were not put on until the score had passed 200 and then proceeded to take 5-56 between them.

Worcestershire's innings ended for 330 at about 4.50pm, leaving Warwickshire two hours' batting, in which time they reached 148-2. The captain Harris and newcomer Venn added 67 for the first wicket before Harris was bowled for 34. Smart did not last long (72-2), but Venn and Burton saw their side safely through to the close, by which time the light was "rather poor". Venn's cutting and off-driving "evoked much enthusiasm" as he advanced to 78*, while Burton's "fine defence" saw him to an overnight score of 28*.

Although Warwickshire's 'other eleven' had not had a bad first day, they were not without their critics. In particular, their bowling came in for censure, notably from the reporter from the *Birmingham Gazette*, who described it as "the most innocuous and inept bowling that even an Edgbaston crowd has seen", and stated that Worcestershire's big total was due not to the strength of their batting but to the weakness of Warwickshire's attack. Strong words, and perhaps a little harsh in view of the late successes of Santall and Smart, and the prematurely cut off promise of Albert Howell. But he was not alone in these opinions, even if others expressed them a little more circumspectly.

Day 2 - Tuesday 5 August 1919

With the Bank Holiday over the weather cheered up, and the forecast for the Midlands was for fair or cloudy weather with moderate or rather high temperatures *(The Times)*. Rain fell overnight at Derby - though not, apparently, at Edgbaston – but play started on time in both games, and proceeded uninterrupted to its conclusion. This was of course the final day of both matches.

At Derby, things quickly went wrong for the home team. After not much more than ten minutes' play they had gone from their overnight 75-1 to a far less healthy 80-4. The overnight rain made the pitch slower but "it had not appreciably affected the surface, so that Derbyshire's collapse was surprising". The previous evening's "fire and dash" was now replaced by a period of retrenchment, but once a stand of 83 between present and future captains John Chapman and Guy Jackson was broken, the collapse resumed, and Derbyshire subsided from 163-4 to 189 all out, made in 3½ hours *(Manchester Guardian)*. Harry Howell (5-65) and Willie Hands (4-36) shared nine of the wickets, but contemporary match reports do not single their bowling out for any special praise. It seems the batsmen were more responsible than the bowlers for Derbyshire's poor second day showing.

Derbyshire, 170 behind on first innings, were asked to bat again; in such a time-limited game, this was surely Warwickshire's only option if they wanted to secure a win. This time two wickets fell quickly, but with most of the batsmen getting some sort of a start "there seemed for the greater part of the afternoon a possibility of the game being saved". But too many batsmen were getting out without making a significant score. Meanwhile George Beet was rooted to the crease: his 50 took two hours as he made virtually a lone attempt to keep alive Derbyshire's hopes of avoiding defeat. He was finally lbw at 136-7, with 34 runs still needed to make Warwickshire bat again. John Corbett and Jim Horsley added 27 for the ninth wicket in 40 minutes.

By the fall of the ninth wicket at 164, time was no longer a serious issue. Unless Horsley and the genuine number 11 Bestwick were able, improbably, to manufacture a seriously long and productive last wicket partnership, there was always going to be time for Warwickshire to knock off the modest number of runs they would need – if indeed they were required to bat a second time at all.

So six runs were still needed to make Warwickshire bat again when the last Derbyshire pair came together. Let the *Birmingham Post* describe the concluding stages of the game:

"Before a run was added, Rotherham had the mortification of failing to hold a sharp chance in the slips offered by Horsley, and the ball sped past him for a couple of runs. Bestwick managed to subscribe to a single, and then a four to Horsley gave Derbyshire the advantage of one run for which they had fought so strenuously. Without addition Bestwick skied to cover point, Warwickshire thus needing two to win. Without delay Bates and Smith went to the crease, and Oliver tossed up a ball which Bates hit to leg for four, and the game was over."

Warwickshire thus recorded their first win of the season, taking 20 wickets in not too much more than a single (long) day's play – although none of the match reports that I have seen give any particular credit to their bowlers, not even Harry Howell with his match figures of 9-107. 'Twas ever thus.

Unfortunately the Warwickshire side at Edgbaston was unable to make it two wins on the same day. In truth, barring an unexpected and sudden improvement in the bowling of one side or the other, there was never any realistic prospect of a result over the two days, and the game with Worcestershire eventually petered out as an aimless draw.

The star of Day 2 at Edgbaston was undoubtedly Harry Venn. Playing his first first-class innings, he started the day on 78 and was missed in the slips early on, but then did not give another chance until he was in three figures. After spending ten minutes on 99, he eventually reached his century after 2¾ hours with a hit over cover for three off Hunt (*Evening Despatch*). He was then twice missed by Turner off difficult chances at mid-off, at 107 and 109[51], before finally falling for 151 made in five minutes under four hours' batting. He hit 18 fours, his most prolific stroke being a square cut which took the ball to the boundary "with great speed".

---

51   This is as reported in the *Birmingham Post*. The *Birmingham Gazette* says that his only chance was a hard hit to mid off when he was 130.

Earlier, his fellow debutant Burton had left at 203 after sharing a partnership of 131 for the third wicket, his own share of the partnership being 47. The character of his innings is reflected in the *Post*'s comment that "no player in the match showed a sounder defence". Venn was fifth out with the score round about 250-260[52], bringing in 16-year-old Reggie Santall who made 15 before being bowled by a man three times his age – not something that happens very often in first class cricket. Luckin[53], Benjamin and Suckling all made useful scores, and Warwickshire went past their opponents' total with two wickets still in hand. When the ninth wicket fell at 391 after a stand of 62 between Luckin and Suckling, the innings came to an end.

Harry Venn, whose innings of 151 at Edgbaston remained the highest by a Warwickshire player making his first-class debut until 1971.

But how, exactly? Most scorecards show the total as 391 all out, with "no. 11 A.L.Howell – absent hurt". But what of young George Tyler? If he was a full substitute, surely he was entitled to bat, or at least to an entry in the scorecard?

For my money the most reliable source for an explanation of the conclusion of Warwickshire's innings is that of the contemporary reporter for the *Birmingham Post*, as being someone with his ear closer to the ground than the writers of any national or, dare one say it, less prestigious local newspapers. He was in no doubt that the innings ended with a declaration, writing on the day "With the score at 391 for nine wickets Harris applied the closure". Moreover, the same paper's scorecard on 6 August gave the final Warwickshire total as follows:[54]

---

52   Reports differ about the score at Venn's dismissal. The *Post* says he was out at 248, while the *Mail* says that Hastilow was fourth out at 248, "and Venn soon followed". From the scorecard, it is not possible that *both* were out at 248, but from analysis of the card, the *Mail*'s version of events looks the more credible.

53   Luckin batted at number eight and made 42*, something that would surely have astonished his pre-war Hampshire colleagues. His record in ten matches for Hampshire between 1910 and 1912 was 14 innings, 7 not-outs, 17 runs with a highest score of 8, for an average of 2.42.

54   The same report and scorecard entry were also included in *Berrow's Worcester Journal* on 9 August.

Ten years after: George Tyler stands behind one of his Edgbaston team-mates, Alec Hastilow, in this extract from a photograph of the Moseley CC team of 1929. (Courtesy of Moseley CC)

"Total (innings closed) 391. G.E.Tyler (sub) did not bat".

The contemporary sources from the Post satisfy me that Tyler was indeed a full substitute, and that he deserves his place in the pantheon of first-class cricketers even though he didn't bat or bowl. But it is unfortunate – for his sake, as well as for posterity's – that his captain did not allow him a bat that afternoon at Edgbaston, particularly as the chances of a definite result were now very slim indeed. Some fuller information on his life and cricket career is given here as a footnote.[55] Particularly from the fact that he did not replace the still-injured Howell in the Warwickshire trial match which followed the Worcestershire game on 6-7 August, I infer that Tyler's drafting into the side on 4 August was opportunistic (he just happened to be there at the time) rather than him being a 'merit selection' as twelfth man. But we cannot be sure.[56]

Instead, Cliff and Shakespeare went in a second time, facing a deficit of 61 runs. They proceeded untroubled, scoring at more than 4 runs an over despite frequent bowling changes (the 38 overs of Worcestershire's second innings were shared between seven bowlers). When 6.30pm came – at least thirty minutes before the scheduled close, if not an hour (details of the scheduled hours of play are uncertain), it was agreed that there was no point in continuing, and stumps were drawn with Worcestershire leading by 101 runs, with all ten wickets still intact. Match drawn.

Summing up
Won 1, drew 1: at least Warwickshire had a considerably better outcome to their 1919 double-header than Surrey had had ten years previously. Their first (and, as it turned out, last) success in the season's County Championship was no doubt special cause for celebration. But in other respects little was gained, particularly from the 'experimental' Worcestershire game. Certainly there were one or two promising performances, particularly Venn's, which prompted the *Birmingham Mail* to comment on 7 August that he "seems destined before too long to secure a trial in the first eleven".

---

55 George Edward Tyler was not without cricketing pedigree or credentials. He was born at Sparkhill, Birmingham on 3 October 1898, the son of George Harry Tyler (b. Colchester 1870), sometime captain of Moseley CC and occasional Second XI player for Warwickshire. Before the Edgbaston game on 4-5 August 1919, local newspapers record G.E. as scoring 65 for Moseley II v Mitchell & Butler's on 17 July, 41 for Moseley II v Stourbridge on 26 July, and 34 for G.H.Tyler's team against F.G.Stephens' team in an (?intra-club) match at Moseley's ground at The Reddings on 2 August. There is no record of him bowling in any of the matches for which I have seen scorecards.

56 Early in 2013 CricketArchive amended its scorecard of the Edgbaston game to match that in the *Birmingham Post,* implicitly acknowledging Tyler's claims to a first-class career. At the same time his CricketArchive biography was amended to credit him as a first-class cricketer.

But the area in which the county side was most in need of finding new talent was in bowling, and in that the Edgbaston game was conspicuously unsuccessful. Neither the retained groundstaff members nor the newcomers to the side did anything with the ball to catch the eye for the future; indeed, quite the reverse, for the side's bowling came in for consistent criticism in the local press. Commenting after the match the *Birmingham Post* noted that "the Warwickshire fielding on the whole was good, and their batting was much appreciated by a fair crowd of spectators, but the game revealed in a striking manner the weakness of their attack". The *Mail* confirmed this conclusion, saying that "no new bowler of promise was discovered ... and the match merely clinched the fact that the present weakness is in attack".

Apart from Venn, the only other newcomer singled out for praise by the local press was Reginald Burton, though frequently the praise was accompanied by faint damns. The *Mail* commented "Another new player to win distinction is RHM Burton of Rugby, an enthusiast, who is making progress as a run-getter". It is good to know of his enthusiasm; but all other reports commented one way or another on his defensive play, which reading between the lines one may interpret as concern that he was over-cautious, or else very limited in his skills: "Burton showed a fine defence in a rather poor light" (*Post*, after Day 1); "No player in the match showed a sounder defence" (*Post*, after Day 2); and the final surely-damning remark from the *Gazette*, after Day 2, which described Burton as "a batsman who has even more stolid patience than Quaife".[57]

All in all, the match at Edgbaston was not hugely successful as a venture for discovering new players to make good the known area of weakness in Warwickshire's Championship XI. But seen in its true context, as part (but only part) of Warwickshire's attempt to identify new talent from within the county, it surely served its purpose, even if no obvious new stars were identified. And it also served to provide Bank Holiday entertainment to "a large crowd" on Day 1 (*Evening Despatch*), and to a crowd of about 1500 people on Day 2 (*Birmingham Mail*) - not an insignificant consideration in this first summer after the Great War, where there was a need to keep the game in the public eye and to provide entertainment for a nation getting ready once again to enjoy itself. Additionally, although it did not uncover any special new talent for the visitors either, the fixture helped to maintain interest in cricket in Worcestershire during that county's bleakest hour. So certainly not a waste of time and effort, then, even if the tangible results were meagre.

WHAT HAPPENED NEXT

The rest of the 1919 season
Warwickshire's next Championship match, a home game against

---

57   Even at club level Burton's batting style was described as 'dogged', as he always kept the ball on the ground and "timed his progress from first ball to century to coincide with tea". His only known six for the Rugby club was made when, after his official retirement, he volunteered his services to a depleted team and, batting at no. 10, hit a ball for two which then went for four overthrows, thereby winning the match. [Information kindly provided by Tim Caven, Rugby CC, October 2012.]

Gloucestershire, began two days after the double-header. None of the players from the Edgbaston game was selected, but after their victory at Derby it was no surprise that the Championship side was unchanged. Had it not been for a delayed declaration, they might have repeated the result: the game ended with the visitors struggling at 51-5, chasing 194.

However, their three remaining Championship matches proved less successful, with defeats in all of them. In their final Championship match, at home to Leicestershire, Warwickshire gave a Championship debut to the most successful of their players from the Edgbaston match with Worcestershire, Harry Venn, who thus became the only one of those making their debuts in that match to play Championship cricket in 1919. Opening the innings with Len Bates, Venn's introduction to the game at this level was brief: he was out for 3 in his first innings and, before the first day was over, out for 25 in his second.

Warwickshire's Championship season thus ended with a record of one win, seven defeats and six draws from 14 matches. For this season, places in the table were decided by the ratio between the number of wins and the number of matches played, and Warwickshire's ratio of 7.14% (one win from 14 matches) left them firmly in 15th and last place in the table.

Warwickshire had one remaining first-class match before their season was over – the return match with Worcestershire at Worcester on 25-26 August. Since their game at Edgbaston, Worcestershire had played out draws with H.K.Foster's XI and with Gloucestershire, with one centurion in each game - Edgbaston absentees Arthur Jewell and Frederick Bowley respectively - while against Foster's XI James Turner had returns of 5-56 and 3-27. The home match with Warwickshire, the first-class status of which has never been seriously disputed, was part of a 'Worcester Cricket Festival' held at New Road in the last week of August.

With no competing Championship match, Warwickshire could in theory have put out their full First XI for the game at Worcester, but they did not do so. Instead they selected "a mixed team of regular players and juniors who are expected to find a place in the eleven as their powers develop" (*Birmingham Post*). Of the Warwickshire XI at Worcester, four were first-team first-choices (Len Bates, Tiger Smith, Mick Waddy and Harry Howell); another four had played in the Edgbaston game with Worcester (Harry Venn, Reggie Santall, Edward Hewetson and Albert Howell); one had played a single Championship match earlier in the season (Albert Gittins); and two were making their first-class debuts (H.C.A. 'Tom' Gaunt and Archibald Harris - the latter was the younger brother of the Warwickshire captain from the Edgbaston game). The Worcestershire side was, on paper at least, significantly stronger than their team at Edgbaston, with some of the less successful players from Edgbaston being replaced by, among others, regular opener Frederick Bowley and the Jewell brothers – Maurice a batsman and useful slow left-armer, and Arthur a wicket-keeper-batsman.

The match was unfortunately spoiled by rain and ended in a tame draw. Worcestershire batted first and made 187 (Harry Howell 6-69), but that was as far as play got on Day 1. On the second day, Warwickshire replied with 145 (Venn scoring 58, the only half-century of the game, and Maurice

Jewell taking a career-best 7-56). Worcestershire added 102-7 declared, and Warwickshire – needing a theoretical 145 to win – finished on 70-2 off 15 overs.

Worcestershire's nine first-class games in 1919 produced three defeats and six draws. Not a great return, but the club evidently felt that they had turned a corner, for at the end of the Cricket Festival on 30 August the Committee announced that they would re-enter the County Championship in 1920.

And onwards ...

Worcestershire's return to the Championship in 1920 saw them finish 15th out of 16th, with only the hapless Derbyshire (17 defeats and one abandonment in 18 matches) below them. Warwickshire were up to 12th for that season, but back almost to the bottom (16th out of 17: Glamorgan had now joined the list of first-class counties) in 1921. There followed a long period in which neither county exactly set the Championship alight, positions in the lower half (and often the lower third) being commonplace for both right up to the Second World War. Until they finished 7th in 1939, Worcestershire's best position in the interwar years was 10th in 1930, while Warwickshire's 8th in 1925 was their only top-half finish until 1933. Fourth place in 1934 proved to be a false dawn, and they were back into the double-figure placings for the last four pre-war years.

There was never any question of repeating the double-header venture from 1919. With Worcestershire back in the Championship, the two counties could arrange full, competitive matches without the need for, or threat of, any doubling-up of dates with other fixtures. From 1920 they resumed the pattern of playing each other twice a season in the Championship, but the days of meeting over the August Bank Holiday were now almost completely behind them. Playing Derbyshire over the holiday, which had perhaps been just an unexpected necessity in the fixture list for 1919, became an established fixture for Warwickshire from then onwards, the tradition only ending in 1959. Meanwhile Worcestershire in 1920 began a tradition of their own of meeting Essex over the holiday.

I said 'almost' in the second sentence of the previous paragraph, because as already mentioned, in 1936 and 1937 the fixture list reverted to its pre-WW1 pattern of Bank Holiday fixtures, and for two years Warwickshire again met Worcestershire over the August Bank Holiday – in 1936 at Edgbaston, in 1937 at New Road. In addition, in 1936 Worcestershire's home fixture with Warwickshire was played over the Whit Monday Bank Holiday, but that was a one-off. In all other seasons, the matches between the two counties appeared in the programme wherever they would fit, rather than being tied to a particular date, or even to a particular month.

As for the players in the Edgbaston game, it has to be admitted that none of them ever achieved any great cricketing triumphs, though some of them had their moments. None ever played in a Test match, or even came close. For two of Warwickshire's debutants, Santall and Smart, the game was the first in lengthy careers in which, however – and without meaning to be unkind – they never rose above the status of 'good, steady county players'. But for several of the others, the Edgbaston game marked the end of their first-class careers, or the end of their careers with the county they represented in that game. Here are some fuller details of (mostly) the later lives of the 23 Edgbaston players, on or off the field.

Harold Benjamin did not play again for Warwickshire. He made a single appearance for Northamptonshire nine seasons later, recording the best bowling figures of his career (3-38 in Gloucestershire's second innings, at Peterborough) before leaving the first-class game altogether.

Reginald Burton, Warwickshire second-top-scorer at Edgbaston, played in no other first-class matches, but appeared in four games for Warwickshire II in their first two seasons in the Minor Counties Championship (1931-32). He had joined Rugby CC in 1914 and remained devoted to the club for the next 66 years. He captained Rugby from 1928 until 1947, and - known to all simply as 'The Head Man' - he thereafter continued to be involved with the club in every possible way, including holding the post of club President from 1950 until his death at the age of 80 in October 1980. He was the last survivor of the Edgbaston game.

Reginald Burton was a stalwart of Rugby CC for the whole of his life. This picture of him and his wife was taken during a match played in 1974 to mark his 60 years with the club. (Courtesy of Rugby CC)

For **William Harris** the game against Worcestershire was his 12th and last first-class match, recorded in the unusual pattern of one in each of 1904 and 1905, and five in each of 1907 and 1919. He is said to have played football as an amateur for West Bromwich Albion, though no-one bearing his name ever played in the club's First XI. He died in Southern Rhodesia (now Zimbabwe) in October 1967.

Alec Hastilow CBE played no further first-class cricket after the game against Worcestershire, but captained Warwickshire II from 1935-47. He was a longstanding Committee member of the club, serving as Hon Secretary, Chairman and finally President. He also became Chairman of the Birmingham Chamber of Commerce, and was the father-in-law of

Pakistan's first Test captain, A.H.Kardar.

Edward Hewetson played no first-class cricket in 1920 or 1921, when he was still at Shrewsbury School, but returned to the first-class game for Oxford University and for Warwickshire in 1922. He made 66 first-class appearances in all, the last of them in 1934. His finest hour as a bowler came when he took 9-33 in an innings for The Rest against the Lord's Schools during the annual Public Schools' Festival at Lord's in 1920. In the 1923 University Match he scored 57 in 25 minutes, batting at number 9.

Albert Howell played the last of his 34 matches for Warwickshire in 1922, before embarking on a successful career in the Minor Counties with Durham. One of his finest achievements was to take 23 wickets for 141 runs for them in two successive matches in 1930 (v Yorkshire II and v Staffordshire). He dismissed Jack Hobbs for 2 in 1927 when playing for Durham v H.D.G.Leveson Gower's XI at Sunderland. He died in 1958, on his 60th birthday.

Verner Luckin was born on 14 February - hence his second forename of Valentine. He made an unbeaten century in a Warwickshire CCC trial match immediately after the game against Worcestershire in 1919, but despite this the game at Edgbaston was the last of his 19 first-class matches. He died at the age of 41 in 1931, the first and youngest of the players in the match to die.

For **Reggie Santall** the game at Edgbaston was the start of a long and honourable first-class career in which he scored nearly 18,000 runs and took close to 300 wickets. He was the only player from the Edgbaston match to make a first-class double-century (201* v Northants at Northampton in 1933), and against the same opponents two years later he scored 173* before lunch on the third day. The 3-33 that he took on debut at Edgbaston remained his best first-class bowling figures until his 120th match, when he took 4-37 against Leicestershire in 1925. He was one of only four players to play first-class cricket in England in every season between the Wars (the others were Ewart Astill, Herbert Sutcliffe and Jack Mercer), and was the only one of those four whose entire first-class career was contained within those interwar years. His brother Jack (J.F.E.) - a professional ice-skater - played eight matches for Worcestershire in 1930, but the two brothers never opposed each other in a first-class match, unlike ...

... **Jack Smart** and his brother Cyril (Warwickshire 1920-22, Glamorgan 1927-46), who opposed each other in two matches in 1935. Jack Smart started his career as a batsman and occasional off-spinner, but for much of the 1930s he was Warwickshire's first-choice wicket-keeper. After retiring in 1936 he became a first-class umpire, and stood in four Tests in 1946 and 1947.

Ernest Suckling was engaged on the Edgbaston staff as a bowler in 1919 and played two wicketless matches for them in that season, but the game against Worcestershire was his last for Warwickshire. He took his only first-class wickets when playing *for* Worcestershire, all of them in the same innings – 4-71 against Lancashire at New Road in 1923, in one of his three matches for the county in 1923 and 1924.

George Tyler played no [other] first-class cricket, but played on for the Moseley club into the 1930s. He died at Edgbaston on 24 February 1976 - not at the cricket ground, but at the nearby Queen Elizabeth Hospital.

Harry Venn scored 151 on his first-class debut, and 58 in the return fixture at Worcester three weeks later. But in a career of 34 matches and 60 innings lasting until 1925 he made only one other first-class score of 50 or more – an innings of 115 against Kent at Catford in 1920.

As for the Worcestershire players -

New Zealand-born **Frederick Abbott** still had a full season in the Malvern XI ahead of him when he made his first-class debut at Edgbaston. The second of his three first-class appearances was also against Warwickshire at Edgbaston, in August 1920; his last was at Sheffield later in the same week, and then no more is heard of him. His performances for Malvern in 1919 were described in *Wisden* as "well up to public school standard", but the following year his school had no more to say about him than that he was "a useful performer".

For a while before the First World War, **Ernest Bale** was regarded the country's second-best wicket-keeper, behind only Herbert Strudwick: it was because his career path was blocked by Strudwick that he had left Surrey for Worcestershire. But like Strudwick, he was no batsman, passing a score of 15 no more than a dozen times in 233 first-class innings. His best score was as high as 43 (v South Africans in 1912), but his preceding 18 first-class innings, and the 11 that followed it, all ended in single figures. He lost his place in the Worcestershire side during 1920, and played no first-class cricket after that season.

Dick Burrows had made his first-class debut in Worcestershire's first-ever first-class match (1899), and was the only professional from the Worcestershire side in that game to be still playing in 1919 - though this was to be his final season. His two first-class centuries (112 in 1907, and 107* in 1914) were both made when batting at number 10, and both against Gloucestershire. His most enduring claim to fame, as contained in the record-books, had come at Old Trafford in 1911 when, in clean-bowling Bill Huddleston, he sent a bail 67 yards and six inches - still the longest recorded flight for a bail in such circumstances. It beat by three yards the previous record, which - remarkably - Burrows himself had set, also at Old Trafford, ten years previously. He was a first-class umpire from 1924 to 1931, standing in a single Test match - the rain-ruined game at Trent Bridge in 1926, which lasted only 17.2 overs, making Burrows the Test umpire with the shortest-ever on-field career at that level.

Rupert Cave-Rogers was another of the 1919 Malvern XI described in *Wisden* as "well up to public school standard", but he disappeared from sight, as a cricketer at least, after the match at Edgbaston in 1919. He was the only member of the Worcestershire XI in this game who played no other first-class cricket.

Alfred Cliff played for Worcestershire in 39 matches between 1912 and 1920, but was a regular first-choice only in 1914 and 1919. Principally a batsman, he occasionally bowled slow left arm, and took eight wickets in his first-class career - but never more than one in a single innings.

Arthur Conway had taken 9-38 and 6-49 for Worcestershire v Gloucestershire at Moreton-in-March in 1914, but these were the only 5WIs of his 31-match, 57-wicket first-class career which ended at the end of the 1919 season. He played 30 games at half-back for Wolverhampton Wanderers in 1908/09 and 1909/10.

James Higgs-Walker's entire first-class career consisted of one match for Worcestershire at Cheltenham in 1913, and the Edgbaston game in 1919. He went into teaching, and was headmaster of Sevenoaks School from 1925 to 1953.

Fred Hunt had joined Worcestershire from Kent in 1898, when Worcestershire were still a minor county, as head groundsman and occasional player. In all he made 53 appearances for the county between 1900 and 1922. He remained as head groundsman at New Road until the end of the Second World War, earning a reputation for his fine batting wickets and immaculate outfields. The outdoor life evidently suited him, and he lived to see his 91st birthday, making him the longest-lived of the players from the 1919 match.

The father and uncle of **Herbert Isaac** had both played for Worcestershire before the First World War, when both were killed in action. Herbert played no first-class cricket after 1919, and later moved to Africa, where he played for the Settlers against the Officials in Kenya in 1925 (when he was out 'stumped' in both innings), 1926/27 and 1932/33. He died at Chisekesi, Northern Rhodesia (now Zambia) in April 1962.

Wing Cdr Harold Shakespeare OBE MC AFC played 26 matches for the county between 1919 and 1931, and reappeared in two matches for Worcestershire II in 1949 when approaching his 56th birthday. He was President of Worcestershire CCC from 1974 until his death in July 1976.

Dr James Turner MC played his last first-class match in 1921. He was later the Bursar of Trinity Hall, Cambridge, and was the father-in-law of Robert Runcie, Archbishop of Canterbury from 1980 to 1991.

DERBYSHIRE v WARWICKSHIRE

Played at County Ground, Derby, August 4, 5, 1919.

Warwickshire won by ten wickets.   (Points: Derbyshire 0, Warwickshire 1)

WARWICKSHIRE

1	L.T.A.Bates	b Bestwick	119	not out	4
2	†E.J.Smith	c Morton b Bestwick	72	not out	0
3	W.G.Quaife	b Bestwick	18		
4	R.L.Holdsworth	c Wild b Morton	8		
5	E.F.Waddy	b Bestwick	3		
6	F.S.G.Calthorpe	b Bestwick	17		
7	G.A.Rotherham	b Bestwick	29		
8	C.F.R.Cowan	b Bestwick	52		
9	*G.W.Stephens	lbw b Morton	4		
10	W.C.Hands	b Bestwick	24		
11	H.Howell	not out	4		
	Extras	b 5, lb 4	9		
			359	(no wicket)	4

FoW (1): 1-137, 2-201, 3-212, 4-215, 5-236, 6-255, 7-282, 8-287, 9-338, 10-359

DERBYSHIRE

1	L.Oliver	b Howell	51	c Rotherham b Hands	10
2	H.Wild	b Hands	21	c Rotherham b Hands	1
3	S.W.A.Cadman	b Hands	6	c Howell b Quaife	30
4	†G.Beet	c Smith b Hands	0	lbw b Howell	50
5	*J.Chapman	b Howell	54	c Stephens b Calthorpe	0
6	G.R.Jackson	st Smith b Quaife	33	c Smith b Howell	11
7	A.Morton	c Stephens b Howell	6	b Howell	16
8	C.J.Corbett	c Smith b Howell	2	c Cowan b Hands	23
9	A.Severn	c Smith b Hands	1	b Quaife	1
10	J.Horsley	lbw b Howell	4	not out	14
11	W.Bestwick	not out	5	c Quaife b Howell	1
	Extras	b 2, lb 4	6	b 6, lb 7, nb 1	14
			189		171

FoW (1): 1-68, 2-76, 3-78, 4-80, 5-163, 6-169, 7-173, 8-175, 9-183, 10-189

FoW (2): 1-8, 2-23, 3-74, 4-75, 5-94, 6-123, 7-136, 8-137, 9-164, 10-171

Derbyshire Bowling

	O	M	R	W		O	M	R	W	
Bestwick	44.2	4	178	8						
Cadman	7	4	8	0						
Morton	37	8	109	2						
Horsley	8	0	55	0						
Oliver					(1)	0.1	0	4	0	

Warwickshire Bowling

	O	M	R	W		O	M	R	W	
Howell	23	6	65	5		20.3	4	42	4	1nb
Calthorpe	12	1	47	0		18	4	33	1	
Hands	17.5	3	36	4		19	2	48	3	
Rotherham	5	1	24	0		6	1	19	0	
Quaife	6	1	11	1		13	7	15	2	

Umpires: G.P.Harrison and J.P.Whiteside.   Toss: Warwickshire

Close of Play: 1st day: Derbyshire (1) 75-1 (Oliver 49*, Cadman 6*).

WARWICKSHIRE v WORCESTERSHIRE

Played at Edgbaston, Birmingham, August 4, 5, 1919.

Match drawn.

WORCESTERSHIRE

1	A.T.Cliff	b Benjamin	21	not out		81
2	W.H.N.Shakespeare	b Hastilow	62	not out		67
3	R.A.C.Rogers	c and b Howell	3			
4	F.Hunt	c Benjamin b Hastilow	35			
5	R.D.Burrows	c Harris b Santall	82			
6	F.J.Abbott	b Santall	42			
7	*J.W.C.Turner	b Santall	0			
8	J.A.Higgs-Walker	b Smart	44			
9	H.W.Isaac	b Smart	4			
10	†E.W.Bale	not out	6			
11	A.J.Conway	b Hewetson	2			
	Extras	b 14, lb 13, w 2	29	b 8, lb 4, w 2		14
			330	(no wicket)		162

FoW (1): 1- , 2- , 3- , 4- , 5- , 6-252, 7- , 8- , 9- , 10-330

WARWICKSHIRE

1	*†W.H.Harris	b Hunt	34
2	H.Venn	c Rogers b Burrows	151
3	J.A.Smart	b Burrows	4
4	R.H.M.Burton	lbw b Hunt	47
5	C.A.F.Hastilow	c Burrows b Hunt	14
6	E.P.Hewetson	b Burrows	6
7	F.R.Santall	b Burrows	15
8	V.V.Luckin	not out	42
9	H.L.Benjamin	c Shakespeare b Conway	23
10	E.Suckling	b Higgs-Walker	39
11	G.E.Tyler		
	Extras	b 1, lb 6, w 4, nb 5	16
		(9 wickets, declared)	391

FoW (1): 1-67, 2-72, 3-203, 4-248, 5- , 6- , 7-285, 8-329, 9-391

Warwickshire Bowling

	O	M	R	W			O	M	R	W	
Benjamin	12	2	48	1			6	0	22	0	
Hewetson	17.3	1	77	1	2w		6	1	30	0	1w
Howell	3	0	5	1							
Hastilow	11	0	56	2		(3)	3	0	16	0	
Luckin	7	0	42	0		(4)	4	1	9	0	
Santall	9	1	33	3		(5)	2	0	11	0	1w
Smart	11	2	23	2		(6)	14	3	49	0	
Suckling	2	0	17	0							
Venn						(7)	3	0	11	0	

Worcestershire Bowling

	O	M	R	W	
Conway	25	2	70	1	1w
Higgs-Walker	16.4	1	69	1	5nb
Hunt	44	6	108	3	2w
Burrows	31	5	88	4	1w
Rogers	5	0	25	0	
Cliff	5	1	15	0	

Umpires: S.Santall and A.Taylor.   Toss: Worcestershire

Close of Play: 1st day: Warwickshire (1) 148-2 (Venn 78*, Burton 28*).
GE Tyler was a full substitute for Warwickshire, replacing AL Howell, who was injured early in the match.

3: Other instances in the British Isles

Although there have been only two instances of a county side playing two simultaneous first-class matches, there have been over two dozen other first-class double-headers in the British Isles - though none have been more recent than 1961. These and some similar instances are detailed in this chapter.

Double-headers by MCC

Before the First World War, MCC matches made up a significant component of the annual first-class fixture list. Between 1865 and 1914, the MCC played at least nine first-class matches in each home season, and usually more: from 1878 until 1908 the figure was usually around 12 or 13, and it reached as many as 16 in 1895 (including one match in Ireland), and 15 in 1882, 1883, 1896, 1901 and 1908. These fixtures generally comprised home and away matches against both Universities, a game or two against any visiting tourists, and the balance against county XIs.

This of course was only a relatively small proportion of MCC's full fixture list, which reached 100 matches for the first time in 1881, and 150 in 1890, before peaking at 196 in 1899.

By its nature, the club did not have a 'First XI', and few players could be regarded as 'regulars' for its first-class matches. For example (and picking a year at random), in 1891 as many as 65 cricketers represented the MCC in the season's ten first-class matches, with only two players appearing in as many as half of them (Roland Pope 6 and William Attewell 5). Also by its nature, the club had more than enough players at its disposal to put out two, or maybe more, sides simultaneously that were strong enough to give a decent match to other first-class teams. So it had no need to try to arrange its fixtures so that its first-class matches did not sometimes coincide.

The result was that between 1878 and 1913 the MCC's fixture lists included as many as 21 occasions when they were scheduled to play two first-class matches simultaneously, including two instances in each of 1882, 1885 and 1895. Here is a list of these instances. The 'Play dates' given here and in similar tables later in this book are those on which play actually took place (except that dates when play was scheduled but none took place because of bad weather are also shown, in brackets). As in all similar tables later in this book, the 'Results' are from the point of view of the double-heading team.

Season	Play dates	Fixture	Venue	Result
1878	17-18 June	MCC v Sussex	Lord's	D
	17-18-19 June	Oxford U v MCC	Oxford (Magdalen)	W
1880	13-14-15 May	Cambridge U v MCC	Cambridge	W
	13-14 May	MCC v Lancashire	Lord's	W
1881	16-17 May	MCC v Sussex	Lord's	W
	16-17-18 May	Oxford U v MCC	Oxford	D

1882	11-12-13 May	Cambridge U v MCC	Cambridge	L
	11-12 May	MCC v Sussex	Lord's	W
1882	25-26 May	MCC v Kent	Lord's	W
	25-26-27 May	Oxford U v MCC	Oxford	L
1883	24-25 May	MCC v Kent	Lord's	L
	24-25-26 May	Oxford U v MCC	Oxford	D
1884	9-10-11 June	Cambridge U v MCC	Cambridge	W
	9-10 June	MCC v Derbyshire	Lord's	L
1885	18-19 May	MCC v Kent	Lord's	L
	18-19-(20) May	Oxford U v MCC	Oxford	D
1885	15-16 June	Hampshire v MCC	Southampton	W
	15-16 June	MCC v Derbyshire	Lord's	W
1889	6-7-8 June	MCC v Kent	Lord's	L
	6-7 June	Oxford U v MCC	Oxford	W
1890	22-23 May	Cambridge U v MCC	Cambridge	W
	22-23 May	MCC v Lancashire	Lord's	L
1891	25-26 May	Ld Sheffield's XI v MCC	Sheffield Park	D
	(25-26 May)	MCC v Yorkshire	Lord's (no play)	--
1894	24-25-26 May	Cambridge U v MCC	Cambridge	W
	24-25 May	MCC v Leicestershire	Lord's	L
1895	20-21-22 May	Dublin U v MCC	Dublin	L
	20-21 May	MCC v Derbyshire	Lord's	L
1895	6-7-8 June	Cambridge U v MCC	Cambridge	L
	6-7 June	MCC v Warwickshire	Lord's	W
1896	15-16-17 June	Cambridge U v MCC	Cambridge	D
	15-16 June	MCC v Warwickshire	Lord's	L
1897	10-11 June	MCC v Derbyshire	Lord's	W
	10-11 June	Oxford U v MCC	Oxford	L
1898	19-(20-21) May	MCC v Notts	Lord's	D
	19-(20-21) May	Oxford U v MCC	Oxford	D
1901	20-21-22 May	MCC v Kent	Lord's	L
	20-21-22 May	Oxford U v MCC	Oxford (Christ Church)	W
1907	2-3-4 Sept	MCC v South Africans	Lord's	W
	2-3-4 Sept	Yorkshire v MCC	Scarborough	W
1913	22-23 May	MCC v Hampshire	Lord's	L
	22-23 May	Oxford U v MCC	Oxford	L

Matches at Oxford were played at The Parks unless stated.

The table reveals some patterns in these fixtures. Almost all of the double-headers featured a game against one or other of the first-class Universities; only the second instance in 1885 featured two matches against county sides. The great majority of the games were played in May or early June, reflecting the fact that the majority of the MCC's first-class matches, and all of the Universities', were generally played in the early part of the season. The Whitsun Bank Holiday also fell in this part of the year, but none of the double-headers took place over the holiday itself (when the counties were usually fully engaged against their regular Bank Holiday opponents), although - coincidentally, so far as I can tell - they were frequently held in the week immediately before or the week immediately after the Bank Holiday. With Lord's as MCC's only home ground, it is no surprise that all of the double-headers featured one home match and one away from home.

Of the 20 instances where play took place in both matches, the MCC side won both games on just three occasions (1880, 1885, 1907) and lost both on two occasions (1895, 1913). There were nine instances when MCC won one and lost one, and six when one or both games ended as draws.

Here as in later chapters I offer some items of statistical interest that occurred in some of these games:

· Future Test cricketer Charles Leslie made 111* for Oxford University on his first-class debut in the game at Oxford in 1881.

· The game at Southampton in June 1885 was the first ever first-class match played at the county ground at Northlands Road. George Davenport (101* for MCC) made the first first-class century at the ground, while Notts and England batsman Billy Gunn, playing for MCC, took 5-37 and 6-48 - the only two 5WIs of his first-class career .

· As the list shows, the scheduled MCC v Yorkshire match at Lord's in May 1891 was abandoned without a ball bowled. So was the reverse fixture in the same season, which was due to be played at Scarborough on 27-28-29 August.

· Frederick Martin of Kent took four wickets in four balls for MCC against Derbyshire in the match in May 1895.

· The match in Dublin in May 1895 was MCC's first-ever first-class match outside Great Britain.

· Frank Druce was left stranded on 199* in Cambridge University's innings in the game at Fenner's in June 1895. (See photo on page 94.)

· Cuthbert Burnup was dismissed for 95 and 93 for Cambridge University in the game in 1896, being out to the bowling of Ranjitsinhji in both innings. This was the first-ever instance of a player making two 90s in the same first-class match. Burnup's previous highest score had been 92, so by the end of the game he had made three first-class 90s without yet reaching three figures. (He finally reached his maiden first-class century against the Australians about two months later, without any other intervening 90s.)

· J.T.Hearne took 9-54 and 6-56 for MCC at Oxford in 1897 - and still finished on the losing side.

· In the 1901 game at Oxford, the euphonious pairing of Frank Hollins (84 at no. 9) and Bernard Collins (83* at no. 11) added 149 for the tenth wicket in the University's second innings. This was wicket-keeper Collins' only first-class match; he had been dismissed for a duck in the first innings, again batting at number 11.

After the First World War, MCC's first-class fixture list at home reduced significantly. The club played only six first-class fixtures in each of 1919 and 1920, only five in each of 1921 and 1922, and just four in 1923 and 1924 – their lowest figure until 1970. The 'irreducible minimum' of fixtures that had now been reached was made up of one early-season game against the tourists, a match at Lord's against each of the Universities in their run-up to the University Match, and the end-of-season fixture against Yorkshire at Scarborough. From 1925 the fixture list began to grow again by the addition of a few games against county XIs, and it sometimes included an away match against either Scotland or Ireland. But a team with the unqualified name 'MCC' never again played more than nine first-class matches in a single English season; in the years after the Second World War the figure was generally between six and eight. In these circumstances, the need to double-up first-class fixtures did not arise again ...

... until the 1950s. In 1948, and in alternate years thereafter, MCC played a first-class match against Ireland at Dublin towards the end of the season, and in the intervening years from 1957 onwards they added an away fixture against Scotland to their programme.[58] The MCC sides for these games were generally weaker than those for the games against the counties, though perhaps on a par with those selected to play the Universities. MCC was of course able to select its elevens having regard to the expected strength of the opposition, and – as a crowd-puller – their XIs would generally include the occasional 'big name' player, though perhaps one whose very best years were behind him.

MCC's first-class fixtures with Ireland and Scotland ended after 1968, but in the meantime the demands created by these fixtures led, in the 1950s and early 1960s, to four further and final instances of MCC first-class double-headers in Britain, as follows – in each case including one match outside England:

Season	Play dates	Fixture	Venue	Result
1950	2-4-5 Sept	Ireland v MCC	Dublin	D
	2-4-5 Sept	MCC v Yorkshire	Scarborough	L
1957	3-4-5 July	MCC v Cambridge U	Lord's	D
	3-4-5 July	Scotland v MCC	Aberdeen	D
1959	24-25-26 June	MCC v Oxford U	Lord's	L
	24-25-26 June	Scotland v MCC	Edinburgh	W
1961	14-15-16 June	MCC v Oxford U	Lord's	D
	14-15-16 June	Scotland v MCC	Greenock	L

---

58   There was no fixture in Ireland in 1962, but this had already been compensated for by the fact that in 1961, for the only time in its history, MCC played away first-class matches in *both* Ireland and Scotland.

Items of interest from these matches:

· The game at Oxford in 1959 was Keith Miller's final first-class match. He took 1-52 in the University's first innings (his last victim being the future star of the Indian 1959 touring team, Abbas Ali Baig), but played no further part in the game after pulling a calf muscle and retiring hurt for 0 in his only innings.

· West Indian Rudi Webster, who later played for Warwickshire, took 7-56 and 4-44 on his first-class debut when playing for Scotland in the match at Greenock in 1961, including a wicket with his first ball in each innings (but dismissing a different batsman each time).

First-class double-headers by other club sides

Over the years, a number of wholly or largely amateur clubs in addition to the MCC have made fleeting appearances in the first-class fixture lists, notably I Zingari (17 first-class matches between 1866 and 1904), the Orleans Club (four matches between 1878 and 1883), the Harlequins (four matches between 1924 and 1928), and the Lyric Club (one match in 1890), But by far the most durable, in terms of their first-class appearances, were the Free Foresters, who played 83 first-class matches between 1912 and 1968. All 83 were against either Oxford or Cambridge University, both of whom they met in first-class matches in each season from 1912 to 1962 inclusive[59], with two further and final first-class matches in 1964 and 1968.

The Free Foresters was (and still is) very much a 'gentlemen's club', in the sense that all its players are amateurs. Founded by Rev W.K.R.Bedford as a wandering club in 1856, its membership was originally limited to gentlemen from the Midlands - though this term was defined rather widely, as the permitted source of Foresters' players extended as far north as the southern parts of Lancashire and Yorkshire, and as far south as Hertfordshire and Buckinghamshire. In 1892 the residential qualification was lifted, as later were restrictions on the total number of club members: it became open to all-comers "provided the Committee considered that they had the right qualifications"[60] [no further comment needed!].

By the late 1920s the Foresters' annual fixture list included around 100 matches, with anything up to six matches on the same day (though none on Sundays: the club had been founded by a clerical gentleman, after all). Then as now, their opponents consisted entirely of "county, university, college, schools, regimental XIs and recognised clubs in desirable localities".[61] From around 1906 they began to field particularly strong sides against the two principal Universities, and from 1912 their matches against these two opponents were recognised by MCC as being of first-class status.

With a large player-base, and the expectation that few club members would play more than a few matches for the Foresters each year, it became

---

59   Except that the 1946 fixture against Oxford was not first-class because it was played 12-a-side

60   Philip Whitcombe and Michael Parsons: *The Free Foresters 1856-2006,* Free Foresters CC, 2006

61   Taken from the Club History page for the Free Foresters at www.ukcricket. org/freeforesters

the pattern that their sides against the Universities each year consisted largely of 'Old Boys' of the University in question, taking the opportunity to revisit their old haunts for a match against the latest crop of students. It also became the pattern that these matches were generally among the last of the Universities' home matches each season[62], before the University squads embarked on their pre-Varsity Match tours. Particularly in the later 1920s, the dates of the Foresters' matches against the two Universities were therefore quite close together: in 1927 the match at Cambridge was from 8-10 June, and that at Oxford on 11-14 June; in 1928 the Cambridge game was on 6-8 June, the Oxford one on 9-12 June.

The inevitable occurred in 1929, when the two matches were arranged to be played simultaneously, starting on 8 June. This presented no difficulties for any of the parties concerned – the Foresters had plenty of players they could call on, and the date fitted comfortably enough into the Universities' fixture lists. Here are the summarised details and memorabilia of the double-header:

Season	Play dates	Fixture	Venue	Result
1929	8-9-10 June	Cambridge U v Free Foresters	Cambridge	D
	8-9-10 June	Oxford U v Free Foresters	Oxford	D

· Hubert Rhys scored 149 on his first-class debut in the Foresters' first innings at Fenner's. In his remaining nine first-class matches (mostly for Glamorgan in 1929 and 1930) he only once passed a score of 35.

· Both the games ended as draws, though neither tamely. At Fenner's, the University had a go at reaching the target of 254 in 120 minutes set by the Foresters' third-innings declaration; they finished on 171-2, with Bryan Valentine scoring 101* in 85 minutes. In The Parks the Foresters bowled Oxford out late on the last day, leaving themselves 95 to win in 45 minutes; the game ended with them on 70-6.

As was usual, the two Free Foresters' sides each had a preponderance of former members of the Universities they were opposing. Nine of the Foresters' side at Fenner's had played first-class cricket for Cambridge University, some recently (two had won Blues in 1928) and some rather earlier (two had won their first Blues as far back as 1904 and 1908 respectively). Among the nine were future Test cricketers Maurice Allom and 'Father' Marriott, the sometime Somerset player and future educationalist Jack Meyer, and A.G.Doggart, father of Hubert. In the Parks, the University was faced by eight former Oxford Blues, among then the erstwhile Worcestershire stalwart G.N.Foster (first Blue 1905) and, of the younger generation, future Test cricketer Errol Holmes whose latest Blue had been won as recently as 1927. Also in the Foresters' side in the Parks was former England captain Johnny Douglas, one of the three non-University players in the XI and apart from Holmes the only past or future Test cricketer in the side.

The Free Foresters' team at Oxford also included our friend from Warwickshire's 1919 double-header, Edward Hewetson. In his penultimate

---

62   The matches were always played at Fenner's or The Parks: as a wandering club, the Free Foresters never played any 'home' first-class fixtures.

first-class match he scored just 2 and 10, and took 0-55 and 1-38. This appearance makes him the third and last cricketer to play in both a county double-header and a club double-header in England.[63]

After 1929 the Free Foresters' matches against the two Universities gradually moved apart on the fixture list. They were a week apart in 1930, three weeks apart in 1931, and nearly a month apart in 1932. For most of the rest of the club's first-class life, the matches were usually one or two weeks apart, with the game at Oxford generally (though by no means always) preceding that at Cambridge. Thus there was never again any instance of simultaneous matches.

1962 was the last season of the regular first-class matches between the Free Foresters and the Universities. The games were played as usual in 1963, in the belief that they were first-class[64], but for reasons I have not been able to establish (could it have had anything to do with the abolition of the amateur/professional distinction after the 1962 season?), they were subsequently ruled by MCC to have been 'not first-class'. This seems to have triggered off some reaction at the Universities, particularly at Cambridge, for in 1964 – for the first time since 1908 – that University had no fixture with the Free Foresters. The Universities alternated fixtures with the Foresters from 1964 to 1967, but in that year Cambridge played their last three-day match against them. Oxford took rather longer to sever the ties, continuing with a three-day fixture in most years until 1983. For some reason, Oxford's matches against the Free Foresters in 1964 and 1968 *were* deemed to be first-class: perhaps this is a bigger mystery than why the other games after 1963 were not.[65]

Simultaneous matches by Festival XIs bearing the same name

Between the Wars and for many years after the Second World War, the English season customarily came to an end with a number of week-long Festivals, held usually in the first or second week of September in seaside resorts such as Scarborough, Folkestone, Hastings, Torquay, and Blackpool. Kingston-upon-Thames[66] was a notable geographical exception. The Festival matches were played 'properly', but in a more relaxed atmosphere than the competitive games of the rest of the season, as they were usually of no wider consequence than providing entertainment for the holiday crowds and, one suspects, for the players as well.

The teams involved in these games were usually scratch sides brought together for the occasion, playing under a variety of names to reflect some

---

63   The only others to do so are Willie Quaife, who played for Warwickshire against MCC in both 1895 and 1896, as well as against Derbyshire at Derby in 1919, and H.D.G.Leveson Gower, who played for MCC against Oxford University in 1898 and against Yorkshire in 1907, as well as in The Oval leg of Surrey's 1909 double-header.

64   They are listed as first-class fixtures in the *Playfair Cricket Annual* for 1963, and included in the principal fixture list printed in *Wisden* 1963.

65   The 1963 matches were retrospectively ruled 'not-first-class' by MCC in July 1963 (see *Cricket Quarterly* Vol 1 no. 4, page 167), but I have not researched any formal rulings for later years. Fixtures between the Free Foresters and Oxford and Cambridge Universities resumed in 1987 and 1988 respectively, though they have not continued in unbroken sequence since those dates, and have generally been one-day games.

66   See note 30 above.

feature that was common to all, or most, of the players in each side, but not to their opponents.[67] These names might have been geographical (North, South, East, West), or social (Gentlemen, Players), or sometimes a combination of the two (e.g. 'Gentlemen of the South'). Or they might have taken the name of the team's organiser (e.g. H.D.G.Leveson Gower's XI, longtime participants at the Scarborough Festival). In later years, as overseas players became more numerous within the county and league ranks, sides were also put together of English-based cricketers who originally hailed from 'anywhere but England', under the name of 'Commonwealth XI'.

The names of these scratch sides were generally titles of convenience only. Unless otherwise stated, I have here used the team-names as given in the match-reports in *Wisden*. Other variations of the accepted team names might equally well have been chosen in at least some cases (e.g. to take a random example, all 22 participants in the Gentlemen v Players match at Folkestone in 1934 played for southern counties, so the match might equally well have been styled as 'Gentlemen of the South v Players of the South'). As we will see shortly, in several cases there is not agreement on team-names in all sources.

In these circumstances there was no prima facie reason why two Festival XIs bearing exactly the same name (as recorded in *Wisden*) should not be playing simultaneously at two different grounds, and there were at least four instances when this happened. In fact in three of these instances, *both* sides in the two games bore the same names.

These four instances are of course quite different from those that have been described in this book so far. In these earlier instances, the double-heading side was representing a defined and established organisation, either a county or a club. In the Festival instances, however, the double-heading sides were not representing anyone apart from themselves, on a one-off basis and only for the duration of the match concerned. The four Festival instances were as follows:

Season	Play dates	Fixture	Venue	Winners
1934	5-6-7 Sept	Gentlemen v Players	Folkestone	Gents
	5-6-7 Sept	Gentlemen v Players	Scarborough	Drawn
1948	4-6 Sept	South v North	Hastings	South
	4-6-7 Sept	South v North	Kingston	Drawn
1952	6-8-9 Sept	South v North	Kingston	South
	6-8-9 Sept	South v Rest of England	Hastings	Drawn
1957	4-5-6 Sept	England XI v Commonwealth XI	Hastings	Eng XI

---

67 To judge from the pre-season fixture lists as published in *Wisden*, it would appear that the team names were decided long before individual players were invited to the Festivals, though it is less clear whether the players were selected in order to fit the team names, or whether the organisers simply fitted the available players to the pre-selected team-names as best they could. For the 'Gentlemen v Players' fixtures, and those involving Commonwealth XIs, the former was no doubt the case, but for other fixtures I am not so sure.

4-5-6 Sept	England XI v Commonwealth XI	Torquay	Drawn

Points of interest:
- The game at Folkestone in 1934 was Jack Hobbs' last first-class match, ending a career that had begun in 1905. The Players' captain, he scored 24 and 18, opening in both innings with Charlie Barnett of Gloucestershire.

- As an example of the geographical imprecision of some of the team names in these games, three players from the surely-southern county of Gloucestershire (Charlie Barnett, George Emmett and Tom Graveney) played for the North side at Hastings in 1948. In the same match Worcestershire's Roly Jenkins played for the South, and his county colleague Reg Perks for the North. The North team contained only one player from an unequivocally northern county – Nigel Howard (Lancashire).

I said "at least" four instances a couple of paragraphs ago, because – as indicated – the naming of Festival XIs seems to have been somewhat flexible. There are as many as eight other instances where the ACS listing of first-class matches, along with that on the CricketArchive website, gives the same name to two simultaneously-playing sides, but *Wisden* does not. As the table of these matches below shows, the differences between the alternative names are trivial. There is almost certainly no indisputably 'correct' name for the teams concerned, so you can either regard these as bona fide double-headers, or as near-misses, according to preference. The team-names in normal type in this table are as given by ACS and CricketArchive; names in italics are variants as given in *Wisden*.

Season	*Play dates*	*Fixture*	*Venue*	*Winners*
1902	1-2-3 Sept	Gentlemen v Players	Scarborough	Drawn
	1-2-3 Sept	Players / *XI Players of England* v Australians	Harrogate	Aust
1904	5-6-7 Sept	North v South	Scarborough	Drawn
	5-6-7 Sept	South / *South of England* v South Africans	Hastings	Drawn
1905	31 Aug , 1-2 Sept	England XI v Australians	Bournemouth	Aust
	31 Aug , 1-2 Sept	England XI / *An England XI* v Lancashire	Blackpool	Tied (scores level)
1947	3-4-5 Sept	South / *South of England* v South Africans	Hastings	SA
	3-4-5 Sept	South v North	Kingston	South
1947	6-8-9 Sept	North v South	Scarborough	Drawn
	6-8-9 Sept	South / *South of England* v Sir PF Warner's XI	Hastings	Warner

1949	3-5-6 Sept	North v South	Scarborough	Drawn
	3-5-6 Sept	South / *South of England* v New Zealanders	Hastings	NZ
1950	2-4-5 Sept	South v North	Kingston	North
	2-4-5 Sept	South / *South of England* v West Indians	Hastings	Drawn
1952	3-4-5 Sept	England XI / *An England XI* v Indians	Hastings	Drawn
	3-4-5 Sept	England XI v Commonwealth XI	Kingston	C'wealth

Snippets from these matches:

· In the game against the South Africans at Hastings in 1904, Gilbert Jessop scored 159* in 120 minutes out of a team total of 237 all out.

· Needing 159 to win in the fourth innings in the match at Bournemouth in 1905, the Australians were 153-6, but their eighth and ninth wickets fell with the scores level, before the last pair scored the winning run. The match aggregated 861 runs for 39 wickets, but the highest individual innings was only 52.

· There was also a close finish in the other game in 1905. Lancashire needed 169 to win after a third-innings declaration, but their seventh wicket fell off the fourth ball of the last over, with the scores level, and at that point the game ended. Under today's laws the result would have been a draw, but under the laws prevailing at the time, it was recorded as a tie.

· On the same dates as the two 'South' sides were playing at Scarborough and Hastings in 1947, a further first-class fixture 'Surrey & Kent v Middlesex & Essex' was being played at Kingston. There was definitely no shortage of opportunities for southern cricketers at the end of that long, hot summer! What is more, of the 22 'South' players at Scarborough and Hastings, 11 were from one of the four counties who were also providing players for the match at Kingston, and six more players from those counties were included in Sir Pelham Warner's XI at Hastings. And yet there was no room for even a single Hampshire player in any of the sides.

· In the North's second innings at Kingston in 1950, Dennis Brookes was dismissed for 171, which took him to exactly 2000 runs for the season.

Near misses

These are of three types: instances where the names of two simultaneously-playing teams were similar but all sources are agreed that they were not identical; instances involving MCC sides that had fuller names than just 'MCC'; and instances involving matches that were not both regarded as first-class matches, but which just might have been.

The first category consists of a single instance in which there is a relatively trivial difference between the names of one of the participating teams, on the same lines as those described in the previous section, but in this case there is unanimity among the principal sources, in that the ACS match-list and CricketArchive both go along with the team-names used in *Wisden*. The instance is as follows:

Season	Play dates	Fixture	Venue	Result
1931	(2)-3-4 Sept	Gentlemen v Players	Folkestone	D
	(2)-3-(4) Sept	Gentlemen of England v New Zealanders	Eastbourne	D

The second category is made up of four instances – again, in end-of-season Festival matches – in which an MCC team was playing in one match, while a team representing the MCC (and including MCC in its name) was playing simultaneously elsewhere. But in all four cases, the latter MCC team was, or was intended to be, a side made up of players from the MCC Test-touring party from the preceding or the forthcoming winter, coming together for a first or a last hurrah, and was named accordingly:

Season	Play dates	Fixture	Venue	Winners
1927	7-8-9 Sept	Kent v MCC	Folkestone	MCC
	7-8-9 Sept	CI Thornton's XI v MCC South African Touring Team	Scarborough	Drawn
1928	5-6-7 Sept	Kent v MCC	Folkestone	MCC
	5-6-7 Sept	CI Thornton's XI v MCC Australian Touring Team	Scarborough	Drawn
1929	11-12-13 Sept	Yorkshire v MCC	Scarborough	Yorks
	11-12-13 Sept	MCC Australian Touring Team v The Rest	Folkestone	Rest
1930	6-8-9 Sept	South v MCC	Folkestone	South
	6-8-9 Sept	Lord Hawke's XI v MCC South African Touring Team	Scarborough	Drawn

The four MCC touring parties in these games were respectively those due to travel to South Africa for the 1927/28 season (the original tour captain Guy Jackson played, before he later had to withdraw from the tour); those due to travel to Australia in 1928/29; again, the 1928/29 Australian tour party, supplemented by opener Patrick Kingsley; and the team due to tour South Africa in 1930/31.

Other MCC tour parties had similar 'home' games in other seasons around this time, but no others of these ever coincided with another MCC fixture.

The third category contains two other near-miss instances that have come to my attention. There may be others like them, but if so I'm afraid they have so far passed me by.

The first is outwardly very similar to the Surrey instance in 1909. In *Wisden* for 1938, the fixture list for the coming season records that on 25 June 1938 Sussex were due to start games against both Kent at Tunbridge Wells and Cambridge University at Hove. Sussex regularly played home matches against one or both of the Universities, so the latter may be regarded as an 'established' fixture.

Its inclusion in the *Wisden* fixture list suggests that the Hove match was regarded as first-class at the time - or at least that it was not, at that stage, definitely *not* first-class. But by the time the season started it had been established – how, I have been unable to find out – that the game was definitely not a first-class match[68], and so it was excluded from the end-of-season averages for 1938. There is no scorecard of it, nor even a potted score, in *Wisden* 1939.[69]

As *Wisden* and many other sources tell us, the match against Kent was a rain-spoiled draw. But details of the match at Hove are more elusive. At the time of writing, the scorecard of the game is not even available on CricketArchive. But fortunately the match was given decent coverage in *The Times* and *The Cricketer*, with detailed reports on all three days of play (25-27-28 June) in the former, and the full scorecards in the latter. A potted score is as follows:

Sussex 116 (V.C.Humphrey 39; W.R.Rees-Davies 4-23, J.V.Wild 4-24) and 329 (G.A.Collins 85, R.G.Stainton 62, J.C.Whitehead 39; M.A.C.P.Kaye 4-80) beat **Cambridge University** 293 (P.A.Gibb 99, N.W.D.Yardley 75, F.G.Mann 41) and 86 (A.G.Tuppin 6-38) by 66 runs.

The Sussex players named in that score may not be too familiar, but there were at least three now-well-known names in their XI - George Cox (junior), bowler John Nye, and an unexpected guest, the 17-year-old South African N.B.F. 'Tufty' Mann. Of the Sussex XI, six had already played first-class cricket for the county, and a seventh (Collins) was to do so the following year. On the other hand, two - Whitehead and Humphrey - never played in a first-class match, while Tufty Mann did not begin his prestigious first-class career for another 18 months, and never played a first-class match for an English county side.[70] The Cambridge side was at full strength, being identical with the XI that drew the Varsity Match a week later.

In a further parallel with the Surrey 1909 instance, Sussex included a 'Grand Old Man' in their team, in the form of 54-year-old John Mathews, who had played 40 matches for the county between 1909 and 1930. One of county cricket's more durable, if not conspicuously successful,

---

68   "The encounter will not be included in averages and has been arranged at the urgent wish of the Cantabs". From *In the Pavilion* by Sir Home Gordon, in *The Cricketer*, 7 May 1938, page 34.

69   *Wisden* 1939 acknowledges the fixture in the summary of Cambridge's matches in 1938, where it gives the result but not any scores, and appends the note "This match was not regarded as a first-class fixture" – a fact confirmed a few pages earlier when *Wisden* expressly states that performances in the match at Hove had been ignored in the preparation of the University averages. (*Wisden* 1939, pp 624 and 612 respectively.) There is no reference whatsoever to the match in the section of the Almanack dealing with Sussex's season.

70   Although George Mann and Tufty Mann opposed each other in this 1938 game, neither dismissed the other in either innings, so unfortunately there was no early instance here of Mann's inhumanity to Mann (to quote John Arlott's fine *bon mot*).

performers, Mathews had a 'second tier' career that lasted 43 years – he played his first Minor Counties match for Wiltshire in 1903 when just past his 19th birthday, and his last match for Sussex Second XI (though not in the Minor Counties Championship) in 1946, at the age of 62.[71]

Sussex's answer to John Shuter. John Mathews played his last game for Sussex Second XI at the age of 62, eight years after representing the county in a near-miss double-header against Cambridge University.

Because the non-first-class status of the match at Hove is not in dispute, I have not sought to follow up the circumstances in which it was arranged, nor whether it was ever contemplated as being a first-class fixture - and if so, how and why that status came to be denied it. But based on the Surrey instance in 1909, it is arguable that there was a case for allowing the match that status even though it was played simultaneously with a Championship match. But evidently that argument was never made.

On the other hand, in the same way that the Surrey instance has been quoted in support of allowing first-class status to the Warwickshire v Worcestershire match at Edgbaston in 1919, the fact that the Hove game in 1938 was not allowed first-class status may perhaps be seen as changing the rules of precedent on this subject, by providing a clear steer that simultaneous matches by teams representing the same county can now no longer both be regarded as first-class. Perhaps.

The second instance in this final near-miss category dates from 60 years earlier, and several hundred miles further north.[72]

Scotland are not regarded by the ACS as playing a first-class match until 1905, though representative Scottish XIs began playing matches at least as early as the 1870s. Between 1874 and 1880, Scotland played only two such

---

71   In his first-class career, Mathews played 61 innings for an average of only 13.64, with a highest score of 78 and just one other score of 50 or more. But to his credit, it should be recorded that in one of his second eleven matches in 1946 he scored 50* when three months past his 62nd birthday, off a Kent attack that included future Test bowler Fred Ridgway.

72   I am greatly indebted to Neil Leitch, the Honorary Historian of Cricket Scotland, for bringing this instance to my attention, and for providing many of the details on which the following paragraphs are based.

matches. Yet remarkably, they were both scheduled for exactly the same dates, from 23 to 25 May 1878.

At the time there was no single governing body for representative cricket in Scotland, and so matches were arranged independently by clubs or individuals. Thus it was that in 1878, Major Dickins – a great supporter and organiser of early Scottish cricket – got together a side to play an England XI at Merchiston Castle School, as a benefit for the school's professional and groundsman John Wright; and at exactly the same time, Grange CC – who at the time were becoming the 'MCC of Scotland' – organised a match against Yorkshire, to be played at the club's ground at Raeburn Place. By the time the clash of dates was realised, it was too late to make any changes, and so both games went ahead, about 4½ miles apart on the west side of Edinburgh.

Although neither is regarded by the ACS as first-class, both matches are regarded by Cricket Scotland as 'cap' games. The side against the England XI included four of Scotland's best players of the time, including leading bowler David Buchanan (of Cambridge University, MCC and pre-first-class Warwickshire), while the England side that opposed them was a strong one, including a powerful Nottinghamshire contingent (among them Arthur Shrewsbury, William Oscroft, John Selby, William Barnes, Wilfred Flowers and Jemmy Shaw). In the game itself, Scotland took a useful first-innings lead before falling to pieces in the second innings. On the third day, rain stopped play with the scores level, but Scotland took the field ten minutes after the advertised finish time in order to allow England to win:

> **Scotland** 170 and 52 (J.C.Shaw 6-15) lost to **England XI** 134 (W.Flowers 59; D.Buchanan 6-43) and 89-3 by seven wickets.

Against Yorkshire the home side contained seven of Scotland's top players, including batsman Leslie Balfour (later Balfour-Melville), Scotland's greatest player of the Victorian era.[73] But they too lost, to a Yorkshire side that included five players who had played for England in the first-ever Test Match about 14 months previously (Tom Armitage, Tom Emmett, Andrew Greenwood, Allen Hill and George Ulyett) as well as other big names in Ephraim Lockwood and George Pinder. Although scheduled for three days, the Yorkshire game was completed in two[74]:

> **Yorkshire** 195 (G.Ulyett 107; J.E.Laidlay 5-55, W.F.Webster 5-78; Ulyett's 107 was made out of 147 runs added while he was at the crease) beat **Scotland** 44 (T.Emmett 5-3, E.Lockwood 4-17) and 83 (A.Hill 4-22) by an innings and 68 runs.

According to Neil Leitch, this Scottish double-header was no more than an unfortunate coincidence. But it is such a remarkable curiosity that it seems well worth a place here, even though neither game is regarded as first-class ...

... Except that Yorkshire CCC *do* regard their match against Scotland as first-

---

73 In November 2011 he was among the first dozen cricketers admitted to Cricket Scotland's Hall of Fame.

74 On the scheduled third day a fill-up, one innings match was played between two weakened Yorkshire and Scotland XIs, which the home side won easily: Yorkshire made 57 (Laidlay 6-18), to which the Scotland XI responded with 110-7, batting on after passing the Yorkshire score.

class (see, for example, the Introduction to Roy D.Wilkinson's *Yorkshire County Cricket Club First-class Records 1863-1996,* Limlow Books, 1997). However, this view was rejected by the ACS when agreeing the list of first-class matches in Britain in the late 1970s, for reasons explained as follows:

"The Yorkshire performances in this game are included in the averages in both Lillywhite annuals and in *Wisden.* The Scottish side was in fact 'Gents of Edinburgh' and as A Scotland XI *[sic]* was playing An England XI on the same date, this Yorkshire match is so obviously below first-class standard that it is not included as first-class. Yorkshire continued to play Scotland in the 1880s, but none of the annuals rank these games as first-class". [75]

Given the ACS's eventual view on the Warwickshire v Worcestershire match at Edgbaston in 1919, and the fact that the Scotland team that faced a virtually full-strength Yorkshire side included many of the country's best cricketers, this conclusion might be open to criticism on grounds of inconsistency and factual inaccuracy. But this is not the place to pursue such a criticism. For even if the ACS conclusion were demonstrated to be unsound, this would not create a new double header, as - rightly or wrongly - there never seems to have been any suggestion that the match at Merchiston Castle School should be considered as first-class.

---

75   *British Isles First Class Matches,* ACS Publications, 1976

4: Other instances involving British teams

MCC on tour

The special nature and role of the Marylebone Cricket Club mean that it should come as no surprise to find that all the instances of double-headers in this chapter involve, one way or another, MCC teams.

Between 1903/04 and 1976/77, England's overseas Test tours were arranged and managed under the auspices of the MCC, and apart from in the Tests themselves the sides played all their tour matches under the 'MCC' label. In addition to the Test tours, between 1905 and 2000 a number of other touring sides have also played (or been scheduled to play) first-class matches under the MCC banner – some of them more, some less, representative of the Marylebone club proper rather than of English cricket as a whole. The latter tours were generally either to 'emerging' cricketing countries, or else were goodwill tours arranged to plug a lengthy gap between scheduled Test tours.

Since 1903/04 there have been four occasions when one MCC tour of each type was undertaken in the same 'winter' season, and two others when two MCC tours of the same type were undertaken. The details are as follows:

Simultaneous first-class tours by MCC sides

Season	Test tours and dates		Other first-class tours and dates	
1911/12	Australia	10 Nov - 1 Mar	Argentina	18 Feb - 3 Mar
1922/23	South Africa	10 Nov - 6 Mar	Australia/NZ	3 Nov - 17 Mar
1926/27	--	--	India etc	19 Oct - 27 Feb
			Argentina	31 Dec - 22 Jan
1929/30	New Zealand	31 Oct - 24 Feb	--	--
	West Indies	1 Jan - 12 Apr		
1963/64	India	3 Jan - 24 Feb	East Africa	2 Nov - 4 Nov
1973/74	West Indies	18 Jan - 5 Apr	East Africa	18 Jan - 20 Jan

The destinations given are those where Test matches (in the left-hand columns) or first-class matches (in the right-hand columns) were played. In some cases, matches were also played in some other countries. The dates are those of the first and last days' play in first-class matches.

As the table shows, the dates of the tours in each season overlapped, except in the case of 1963/64. And sure enough, in each of the other five seasons matches in the different tours were arranged to be played on exactly the same dates, or on overlapping dates. In all, 13 pairs of simultaneous or overlapping matches were arranged in which both MCC sides were due to play under that name:

Season	Play dates	Fixture	Venue	Result
1911/12	16-17-19-20 Feb	New South Wales v **MCC**	Sydney	W
	18-19-20 Feb	Argentina v **MCC**	BA (Hurlingham)	L
1922/23	10-11-13 Nov	South Australia v **MCC**	Adelaide	L

	10-11-13 Nov	W Province v **MCC**	Cape Town	W
1922/23	17-18-20 Nov	Victoria v **MCC**	Melbourne	L
	18-20-21 Nov	E Province v **MCC**	Port Elizabeth	W
1922/23	24-25-27 Nov	New South Wales v **MCC**	Sydney	L
	25-27 Nov	Border v **MCC**	East London	W
1922/23	15-16-(18) Dec	Auckland v **MCC**	Auckland	D
	16-18-19 Dec	Transvaal v **MCC**	Johannesburg	D
1922/23	12-13-15 Jan	Otago v **MCC**	Dunedin	W
	12-13-15 Jan	Natal v **MCC**	Pietermaritzburg	W
1922/23	2-3-5 Feb	New Zealand v **MCC**	Wellington	W
	3-5-6 Feb	Transvaal v **MCC**	Johannesburg	W
1922/23	2-3-5 Mar	New South Wales v **MCC**	Sydney	D
	3-5-6 Mar	W Province v **MCC**	Cape Town	W
1926/27	31 Dec-1-(2) Jan	Argentina v **MCC**	BA (Hurlingham)	D
	31 Dec-2-3 Jan	All India v **MCC**	Calcutta	W
1926/27	8-9-10 Jan	Argentina v **MCC**	BA (Belgrano)	W
	9-10 Jan	Rangoon Gymkhana v **MCC**	Rangoon	D
1929/30	31 Dec-1-2 Jan	Otago v **MCC**	Dunedin	W
	1-2-3-4 Jan	Barbados v **MCC**	Bridgetown	D
1929/30	8-10-11 Feb	Auckland v **MCC**	Auckland	D
	10-11-12-13 Feb	British Guiana v **MCC**	Georgetown	W
1973/74	(18-19-20 Jan)	Windward Islands v **MCC**	Castries (no play)	--
	18-19-20 Jan	East Africa v **MCC**	Nairobi	W

BA - Buenos Aires.

Highlights from these matches:

· In the game at Sydney in February 1912, Syd Gregory carried his bat for 186* in NSW's second innings of 403. Jack Hobbs took 4-25 in this innings, unexpectedly outbowling his opening partner Wilfred Rhodes (0-45), who however made up for it by scoring 119 and 109 in MCC's two innings.

· In the simultaneous match at the Hurlingham club in Buenos Aires, MCC's numbers 10 and 11 Rockley Wilson (67*) and Eric Hatfeild (39) added 106 for the last wicket, in an all-out total of 186. One of their team-mates in this game was Morice Bird, veteran of Reigate 1909.

· At Wellington in February 1923, the top-score in MCC's only innings was 130 by New Zealander Tom Lowry, making his maiden first-class century when playing against the country he was later to captain.

- Henry Marshal scored a century (105) on his first-class debut for Argentina in the game at Hurlingham over the New Year of 1927. Although sharing the unusual spelling of his surname, he is not related to the Alan Marshal who played for Surrey in 1909.

- Frank Woolley scored 132 and took 6-50 and 4-38 at Dunedin over the New Year of 1930, to record the sixth and last 'match double' of his first-class career.

- Patsy Hendren made scores of 223* and 254* for MCC in the games at Bridgetown and Georgetown (respectively) in 1930.

- Edward Benson was dismissed 'handled the ball' for MCC in the match at Auckland in February 1930, though there was doubt at the time as to whether he actually touched the ball.

- The programmed double-header in January 1974 sadly did not come about because rain prevented play on any of the three scheduled days at Castries. The match at Nairobi, with which it was due to be simultaneous, marked the only first-class appearance of J.L. (John) Hutton, son of Len and younger brother of Richard: he scored 12 and 39 batting at number 7, and – opening the bowling - took 1-32 and 1-15.

Double-heading in Test cricket

MCC on tour did not always play as 'MCC', of course: in Test Matches they were 'England'. So as well as the dozen or so instances of simultaneous tour matches by sides styled as 'MCC', there is also the possibility, on simultaneous Test tours, of England playing a Test Match double-header. As the above listing indicates, the only chance for this to have occurred was in 1929/30.

At the time, the status of the representative matches in New Zealand and the West Indies in 1929/30 was not 100% clear. Even *Wisden* in 1931 was not consistent. In its reports of the tours, the games in New Zealand were called 'Test matches', but those in the West Indies were referred to simply as 'representative matches', with the visiting team styled 'MCC Team' rather than 'England'; yet Andrew Sandham's 325 in the 'representative match' at Kingston in 1929/30 is listed in the records of 'Great Individual Scores' as having been made for "England v West Indies".[76]

It required the involvement of one of the leading statisticians of the day, E.L.Roberts, to secure consistency of approach to the 'representative matches' in the West Indies in 1929/30.[77] Thanks to his intervention, by the end of the 1930s those matches had finally and definitively entered the canon of Test matches, and as a result the visiting side was finally and definitively styled 'England' – whether or not that was how it was known when the games were actually played.

So, having agreed that 'England' did indeed make simultaneous Test tours in 1929/30, were there occasions when games now styled as Test matches were scheduled for the same dates on both tours?

---

76   *Wisden* 1931 part 1 page 145.
77   See correspondence in *The Cricketer* 1938, on pages 30 and 63

The answer is yes – there were two such occasions. These were therefore the only two pairs of Test matches ever to be played simultaneously by the same country:

Season	Play dates	Fixture	Venue	Winners
1929/30	10-(11)-13 Jan	New Zealand v **England** (1)	Christchurch	England
	11-13-14-15-16 Jan	West Indies v **England** (1)	Bridgetown	Drawn
1929/30	21-22-24 Feb	New Zealand v **England** (4)	Auckland	Drawn
	21-22-24-25-26 Feb	West Indies v **England** (3)	Georgetown	WI

Figures in brackets in the 'Fixture' column indicate the number of the Test within the series.

Highlights of the matches:

- The Christchurch Test of January 1930 was New Zealand's first official Test match. They were captained by Tom Lowry (see the previous set of 'Highlights'). With NZ's first innings score at 21-3, Test debutant Maurice Allom took four wickets in five balls, including a hat-trick.

- The Test at Bridgetown was West Indies' first home Test match. Opener Clifford Roach scored their first-ever Test century (122 in the first innings), but his performance was upstaged by that of 20-year-old debutant George Headley, who scored 21 and 176. For England, leg-spinner Greville Stevens took 10-195 in the match: these made up exactly half of the wickets that he took in his 10-match Test career.

- Geoffrey Legge, who had aggregated only 103 runs in his previous four Test matches, scored 196 in 280 minutes in England's first innings at Auckland. He made a duck in the second innings, and played no further Test cricket.

- At Georgetown, it was again the Roach and Headley Show: Roach overtook Headley's 176 by recording West Indies' first ever Test double-century (a score of 209), while Headley made 114 and 112 in his two innings.

As the above table shows, there were four dates during these matches when play took place in both games: 13 January and 21-22-24 February. A mildly intriguing question that arises is whether, allowing for the time differences between the Caribbean and the South Pacific, there was any point at which two 'England' Test matches were actually in play simultaneously. Disappointingly, the answer is that there wasn't - there were some hours between the close of play in one venue and the start of play in the other.[78] Shame!

---

78   Hours of play in the Caribbean were approximately 10.30 am to 5.30 pm local time (1430-2130 GMT), and in New Zealand approximately 11.30 am to 6.30 pm local time (2330-0630 GMT, including allowances for the daylight saving arrangements that were in operation in New Zealand at this time).

Near misses

Because the 'MCC' touring sides played under a different name in Test matches, I have had to exclude those instances when one touring MCC side was playing a first-class fixture as 'MCC' against a local XI, while another touring MCC side was playing a Test match elsewhere as 'England'. Instances thus excluded are as follows:

England v South Africa (Johannesburg, 1st Test) and MCC v Canterbury (Christchurch), both in 1922/23. Both games started on 23 December 1922; simultaneous playing dates were 23 and 26 December.

England v South Africa (Cape Town, 2nd Test) and MCC v New Zealand (Wellington) 1922/23. The game in New Zealand started on 30 December 1922, and that in South Africa on 1 January 1923; simultaneous playing dates were 1 and 2 January.

England v South Africa (Durban, 5th Test) and MCC v Auckland (Auckland) 1922/23. The Test match started on 16 February 1923 and the game in New Zealand on 17 February; simultaneous playing dates were 17 and 19 February.

England v New Zealand (Wellington, 2nd Test) and two matches between MCC and Trinidad at Port of Spain in 1929/30. The Test Match was played on 24-25-27 January 1930, with the Trinidad games on 22-23-24-25 January and 27-28-29 January respectively. Simultaneous playing dates were therefore 24, 25 and 27 January.

England v New Zealand (Auckland, 3rd Test) and MCC v British Guiana (Georgetown) 1929/30. The Test Match was due to start on 14 February 1930, but play was only possible on 17 February, which was also the second day of the game in Georgetown.

Before the MCC took over responsibility for major tours, matches by touring XIs from England were generally played under the names of their respective tour-organisers. This being so, even if two tours took place simultaneously, there was no chance of any simultaneous matches involving two sides both with the same name. Nevertheless, for completeness mention should be made of the one other season when two separate 'England' sides played Test cricket, although neither side was known simply as 'England' when the Test matches themselves were being played.

We are talking here of 1891/92, when a side under the auspices of Lord Sheffield and captained by W.G.Grace toured Australia, the first and last playing days of the tour being 20 November 1891 and 28 March 1892; while a side led by Walter Read (of Reigate fame) toured South Africa playing matches from 19 December 1891 until 23 March 1892. The former played three games which have come to be accepted as Test matches – at Melbourne on 1-6 January 1892, at Sydney on 29 January-3 February, and at Adelaide on 24-28 March. In South Africa, Read's team played just a single Test,[79] on 19-22 March at Cape Town. This was the only eleven-a-side, and hence the only first-class, match of Read's tour.

---

79   The game was not styled as a Test match at the time, but has since been accepted into the ranks of Test matches.

The dates of the two Test 'series' thus overlapped, with the game in South Africa being played between the second and third Tests in Australia; but the actual playing days of the Tests in the two countries did not. You may want to remember this instance in case you are ever challenged with the quiz question about when England won two Test matches in the course of a week, both by an innings. The Cape Town game was won by an innings and 189 runs on Tuesday 22 March 1892, and that at Adelaide by an innings and 230 runs six days later on Monday 28 March. Then again, you may not ...

A final batch of 'near misses' by English teams abroad also deserves a mention. These were the occasions in the days of private tours when two touring teams from England, each named after their sponsors, manager or captain and therefore each bearing a different name from the other, played first-class matches simultaneously - sometimes in the same part of the world as each other, sometimes not. These instances were as follows.

In 1887/88, two separate touring teams went to Australia and played full programmes of matches between October/November and March. Most of their matches were not first-class, but they still managed to coincide some of their first-class engagements: on 11 November G.F.Vernon's XI were completing a match against Victoria at Melbourne just as A.Shrewsbury's XI were starting a game against New South Wales at Sydney, while on 9-10-12-13 March Vernon's XI's return game against Victoria exactly coincided with Shrewsbury's XI's match against an Australian XI at Sydney.

In 1891/92 (see above), the last day of play in the match between Lord Sheffield's XI and Victoria at Melbourne - 19 March - was also the first day of play in the Test match in South Africa.

In 1894/95 a weak team led by R.S.Lucas made the first-ever tour by a British side to the West Indies, at the same time as Andrew Stoddart's team was winning a Test series in Australia. There were four dates on which both sets of tourists were playing first-class matches: 4-5 March (Lucas's side against All-Trinidad; Stoddart's against Australia in the decisive Fifth Test at Melbourne), and 30 March-1 April (Lucas v All-Jamaica, Stoddart's side v South Australia).

In 1896/97, both Lord Hawke and Arthur Priestley led rather stronger sides to the West Indies. Their teams played simultaneous first-class matches on 25-26-27 February (Hawke v Barbados, Priestley v Trinidad) and on 27-29 March (Hawke v British Guiana, Priestley v Jamaica).

In 1901/02 England were once again in Australia while a weak amateur side, captained by R.A.Bennett, was touring in the West Indies. This time there were seven dates when both sides played simultaneous first-class matches: 22-23 January (when Bennett's side played Barbados while the Third Test was under way at Adelaide), 14-15 February (Bennett v Jamaica, Archie MacLaren's side v Australia at Sydney), 22 February (Bennett v a Combined XI at Kingston, MacLaren v Victoria), and 14-15 March (Bennett v Trinidad, MacLaren v South Australia).

In 1924/25, while England were failing to regain the Ashes in Australia, a strong 'second eleven' was playing a full tour in South Africa. The tour was sponsored by the Anglo-South African financier Solomon (Solly) Joel, and games against provincial sides were played under the name of 'S.B.Joel's XI'. Five representative matches were also played against more or less the full South African Test side, and at the time "there was considerable debate on the subject of the 'Test matches' which were to be played on the tour. In the end it was generally agreed that these could not be official 'Tests' since England could not have a representative eleven in two countries at the same time".[80] An interesting contrast with the outcome of a similar debate about matches five seasons later, but let that pass. Of interest for the present work is that, if the representative matches *had* been accepted as Test matches, it would have created a further instance of simultaneous Tests by the same country, since matches between England and Australia, and between England and South Africa, would have been in progress simultaneously on 23-24-26 December (at Sydney and Johannesburg respectively), on 1-2-3-5 January (at Melbourne and Durban), and on 16 January (at Adelaide and Cape Town). But as it was, the side in South Africa kept its title of 'S.B.Joel's XI' for these games too, so the double-header didn't happen. Ten of the eleven other first-class matches on Joel's tour had at least one playing day that coincided with a day when the English tourists in Australia, as 'MCC', were also playing a first-class match.

---

80   Peter Wynne-Thomas: *The complete history of cricket tours at home and abroad*, Hamlyn, 1989

5: Australia - First home of the geographical double-header

Inter-state double-headers

When the competition for the Sheffield Shield began in December 1892, only three states (or colonies, as they then were) took part - New South Wales, Victoria and South Australia. But first-class cricket had already been played in one of the other Australian colonies - in Tasmania, where Australian first-class cricket began with a game against Victoria at Launceston in February 1851. Before the 1892/93 season was out, two other colonies had also made their first-class debuts, Western Australia playing its first game at Adelaide at the end of March 1893, and Queensland following a week later with a match at Brisbane against New South Wales.

Because of their distance from the main centres, as well as the lower standard of their cricket, these other states were not deemed to be of the same status as the 'Big Three', and they each had to wait their turn before being admitted to the Shield competition - Queensland in 1926/27, Western Australia in 1947/48, and Tasmania in 1977/78.

In its pre-Shield days, Western Australia's first-class cricket consisted largely of matches by the state side on occasional tours eastwards, later supplemented by visits from overseas Test tourists. Meanwhile first-class cricket in the two more easterly non-Shield states was kept alive by means of regular contests against their nearest neighbours - Queensland with NSW, and Tasmania with Victoria - with occasional matches against the other 'Big Three' states. From the mid-1890s a pattern developed, no doubt designed to maximise attendances and thus receipts, of NSW and Victoria playing matches against the 'junior states' over a holiday period - either the Christmas/New Year period, or else the Australia Day holiday towards the end of January.

But if these dates were the most lucrative for the matches against junior states, they were also the best dates for playing Sheffield Shield matches. And so on Australia Day in 1894 the almost-inevitable double-heading began when Victoria played NSW in a Shield game at Sydney, while at the same time putting out a side against Tasmania at Melbourne. Double-heading by sides representing the same geographical entity thus began in Australia over 15 years before the first instance in England.

The first-class status of matches between the Big Three states and their junior rivals was confirmed in 1908 when the Big Three agreed that all interstate matches should be ranked as first class.[81] No exception to this principle was stipulated for matches when one of the participating states was not at full strength, or was playing in another first-class match elsewhere.

The Australia Day game in 1894 was the first of 43 double-headers in Australia, the last of which took place in January 1957. Here are the details of these instances, with the double-heading team in bold type, and the results expressed in terms of the double-heading side:

---

81   Chris Harte: *A History of Australian Cricket*, Andre Deutsch, 1993, pp 232-233.

Season	Play dates	Fixture	Venue	Result
1893/94	26-29-30 Jan	NSW v **Victoria**	Sydney	L
	26-27-29 Jan	**Victoria** v Tasmania	Melbourne	W
1894/95	25-26-28-29-30-31/1	NSW v **Victoria**	Sydney	W
	26-28-29-30 Jan	Tasmania v **Victoria**	Hobart	L
1895/96	25-27-28-29-30 Jan	NSW v **Victoria**	Sydney	W
	25-27 Jan	**Victoria** v Tasmania	Melbourne	L
1897/98	22-25-26-27 Jan	NSW v **Victoria**	Sydney	W
	22-24-25 Jan	**Victoria** v Tasmania	Melbourne	L
1898/99	26-27-28-29 Jan	NSW v **Victoria**	Sydney	L
	26-27-28-30 Jan	Tasmania v **Victoria**	Hobart	L
1899/00	26-27-29-30-31 Jan	NSW v **Victoria**	Sydney	L
	26-27-29-30 Jan	**Victoria** v Tasmania	Melbourne	W
1902/03	26-27-29 Dec	Victoria v **NSW**	Melbourne	W
	26-27-29-30 Dec	**NSW** v Queensland	Sydney	W
1902/03	24-26-27-28-29 Jan	NSW v **Victoria**	Sydney	L
	24-26-27-28 Jan	**Victoria** v Tasmania	Melbourne	L
1903/04	26-28-29-30-31 Dec	Victoria v **NSW**	Melbourne	L
	26-28-29-30 Dec	**NSW** v Queensland	Sydney	W
1904/05	24-26-27-28 Dec	Victoria v **NSW**	Melbourne	W
	24-26-27 Dec	**NSW** v Queensland	Sydney	W
1904/05	27-28-30-31/1-1 /2	NSW v **Victoria**	Sydney	L
	28-31 Jan-1 Feb	**Victoria** v Tasmania	Melbourne	W
1905/06	15-16-18 Dec	**NSW** v Queensland	Sydney	W
	15-16-18 Dec	S Australia v **NSW**	Adelaide	W
1907/08	26-30-31 Dec	Victoria v **NSW**	Melbourne	W
	26-27-28-30 Dec	**NSW** v Queensland	Sydney	W
1909/10	26-27-29 Jan	NSW v **Victoria**	Sydney	L
	29-31 Jan-1-2 Feb	**Victoria** v Tasmania	Melbourne	W
1910/11	24-26-27-28 Dec	Victoria v **NSW**	Melbourne	L
	24-26-27 Dec	**NSW** v Queensland	Sydney	L
1912/13	24-25-27-28 Jan	NSW v **Victoria**	Sydney	L
	24-25-27-28-29 Jan	**Victoria** v Tasmania	Melbourne	L
1914/15	29-30 Jan-1 Feb	**Victoria** v Tasmania	Melbourne	W
	29-30 Jan	Queensland v **Victoria**	Brisbane	W
1920/21	18-19-21-22 Feb	**NSW** v MCC	Sydney	D
	19-21-22 Feb	Queensland v **NSW**	Brisbane	W

1923/24	26-27-28-29-31/12-1/1	Victoria v **NSW**	Melbourne	L
	31 Dec-1-2 Jan	**NSW** v Queensland	Sydney	D
1924/25	21-22-24-25 Nov	**NSW** v MCC	Sydney	L
	22-24-25 Nov	Queensland v **NSW**	Brisbane	L
1925/26	26-28-29-30-31 Dec	Victoria v **NSW**	Melbourne	W
	26-28-29 Dec	**NSW** v Queensland	Sydney	D
1926/27	25-26-27 Jan	**Victoria** v Tasmania	Melbourne	W
	26-27-28 Jan	NSW v **Victoria**	Sydney	L
1927/28	23-24-26-27 Dec	Victoria v **NSW**	Melbourne	L
	24-26-27 Dec	**NSW** v Tasmania	Sydney	W
1927/28	30-31 Dec-2-3 Jan	**Victoria** v South Australia	Melbourne	L
	31 Dec-2-3 Jan	Tasmania v **Victoria**	Hobart	W
1929/30	26-27-28-39-31 Dec	**Victoria** v NSW	Melbourne	D
	26-27 Dec	Tasmania v **Victoria**	Hobart	D
	31 Dec-1-2 Jan	Tasmania v **Victoria**	Launceston	W
	1-2-3-4-6 Jan	**Victoria** v South Australia	Melbourne	W
1929/30	14-15-17 Feb	South Australia v **Victoria**	Adelaide	W
	17-18-19 Feb	**Victoria** v Tasmania	Melbourne	W
1930/31	24-26-27-28 Jan	NSW v **Victoria**	Sydney	D
	24-26-27 Jan	Tasmania v **Victoria**	Launceston	D
1930/31	20-21-23-24 Feb	South Australia v **Victoria**	Adelaide	D
	23-24-25 Feb	**Victoria** v Tasmania	Melbourne	D
1931/32	24-26-28-29 Dec	**Victoria** v NSW	Melbourne	W
	25-26-28 Dec	Tasmania v **Victoria**	Hobart	W
1933/34	22-23-26-27 Dec	**Victoria** v NSW	Melbourne	D
	23-25-26-27 Dec	Tasmania v **Victoria**	Hobart	W
1933/34	29-30 Dec-1-2 Jan	**Victoria** v South Australia	Melbourne	W
	29-30 Dec-1 Jan	Tasmania v **Victoria**	Launceston	D
1935/36	31 Dec-1-2 Jan	Tasmania v **Victoria**	Launceston	L
	1-2-3-4 Jan	**Victoria** v South Australia	Melbourne	D
1935/36	21-22-24-25 Feb	South Australia v **Victoria**	Adelaide	L
	24-25-26 Feb	**Victoria** v Tasmania	Melbourne	W
1938/39	23-24-26-27 Dec	**Victoria** v NSW	Melbourne	W
	26-28 Dec	Tasmania v **Victoria**	Launceston	D

1938/39	30-31 Dec-2-3 Jan	**Victoria** v South Australia	Melbourne	D
	30-31 Dec-2 Jan	Tasmania v **Victoria**	Hobart	W
1946/47	25-26-27-28 Dec	Tasmania v **Victoria**	Launceston	D
	26-27-28-30 Dec	**Victoria** v NSW	Melbourne	W
	30-31 Dec-1 Jan	Tasmania v **Victoria**	Hobart	D
1948/49	24-27-28-29 Dec	**Victoria** v NSW	Melbourne	D
	25-27-28-29 Dec	Tasmania v **Victoria**	Hobart	D
1948/49	31 Dec-1-3-4 Jan	**Victoria** v South Australia	Melbourne	D
	31 Dec-1-3 Jan	Tasmania v **Victoria**	Launceston	W
1953/54	26-28-29-30 Dec	**Victoria** v NSW	Melbourne	L
	26-28-29 Dec	Tasmania v **Victoria**	Hobart	D
1953/54	31 Dec-1-2 Jan	Tasmania v **Victoria**	Launceston	L
	1-2-4-5 Jan	**Victoria** v South Australia	Melbourne	W
1956/57	18-19-21-22 Jan	Queensland v **Victoria**	Brisbane	D
	22-23-24 Jan	**Victoria** v Tasmania	Melbourne	W

Victoria were the side doubling up in 32 of these instances. All of these involved one match against Tasmania, generally around the Australia Day holiday up to 1926/27, and in the Christmas/New Year period thereafter. In 20 of these instances Victoria's 'senior' opponent was NSW, and in ten it was South Australia. That leaves two instances, in 1914/15 and 1956/57, when both their opponents were 'junior states' (Tasmania and Queensland, although by 1956/57 Queensland were no longer a true junior, and the match at Brisbane was a Sheffield Shield fixture). On both these latter occasions, Victoria put out their full First XI for the match against Queensland – inevitably so for the Shield match in 1957, less predictably for the game in January 1915 – but on both occasions their residual 'Second XI' was strong enough to beat Tasmania comfortably.

In the other 11 instances the double-heading side was New South Wales, their opponents in the more junior match being Queensland on ten occasions and Tasmania just once, in 1927/28. All these instances were played over the Christmas holiday period, with the exceptions of two instances when the senior NSW side was playing against MCC at Sydney while a 'Second XI' was playing Queensland at Brisbane (1920/21 and 1924/25), and a third instance (in 1905/06) which occurred in mid-December, when NSW's Sheffield Shield opponents were South Australia rather than their holiday-season opponents of Victoria.

Victoria's instances in January 1895, January 1899 and January 1931 are notable because both of the state's simultaneous matches were played away from home. There are no comparable instances among NSW's 11 double-headers; neither were there any instances in Australia when the double-heading side has been at home in both its matches (as was the case – uniquely so far in this study - with Surrey in 1909).

Here are the usual highlights associated with the double-header matches in Australia:

- Among the well-known or Test cricketers who made their first-class debuts in these matches were Warwick Armstrong, E.F. 'Mick' Waddy (later of Warwickshire, who played against Derbyshire in their 1919 double-header), 'Sunny Jim' Mackay, Ranji Hordern, Bill Whitty, Ted a'Beckett, Ben Barnett, Ernie McCormick, Leo O'Brien, Jack Badcock, Chuck Fleetwood-Smith, Ian Johnson and Neil Harvey. Badcock was still two months short of his 16th birthday when he made his debut for Tasmania v Victoria in February 1930; he was dismissed 'stumped' in both innings.

- Future commentator Alan McGilvray and future Test cricketer Doug Ring were among those making their first-class debuts in the more senior match of a pair of double headers – McGilvray for NSW v Victoria in December 1933, and Ring for Victoria v NSW in December 1938.

- Charles Eady was Tasmania's star performer in some of the earlier matches in the list. In January 1895 he scored 116 and 112* in the match against Victoria – the first instance of a player scoring two centuries in a first-class match in Australia. A year later his bowling came to the fore, with figures of 8-34 and 4-29, and in the same fixture two years later he took 7-57 and 5-104. A year later still (January 1899) he scored 92 and 31 and took 7-66 and 5-63, to record the 'match double' - a feat previously achieved in Australia only by George Giffen.

Outstanding performances with bat and ball for Tasmania in the 1890s earned Charlie Eady (left) two Test appearances, but like Jack Badcock (right) he could not reproduce his domestic form at international level.
In 12 Test innings, Badcock made one century and 11 single-figure scores.

- The only double-century made for a 'junior' side in the 43 pairs of double-headers was an innings of 274 by Jack Badcock, now aged 19, for Tasmania against Victoria in December 1933; he also made 71* in Tasmania's second innings. Badcock went one step further when playing in a double-header match in February 1936: now playing for South Australia, he made a score of 325 against Victoria at Adelaide.

· Other batting notes: Reg Hawson was left 199* in Tasmania's second innings against Victoria in January 1913 ... in the simultaneous match at Sydney, Victor Trumper (138) and Eric Barbour (146) added 270 for NSW's eighth wicket – still the Australian record partnership for this wicket ... Roy Lonergan scored 115 and 100 for South Australia v Victoria in December 1933 ... Percy Beames made scores of 226* and 169* for Victoria in their two matches against Tasmania over Christmas and New Year 1938/39.

· NSW bowlers took a hat-trick in each of their simultaneous games in December 1902: on Boxing Day, Warwick Armstrong performed the feat in Victoria's first innings at Melbourne, while on 29 December Thomas Howard repeated it to end Queensland's second innings in the match at Sydney (he actually took the last four Queensland wickets in five balls).

· Other bits and pieces: The NSW v Victoria match in January 1895 was the first Sheffield Shield match, and only the second first-class match anywhere, to extend into a sixth day of play ... Tasmania's win over Victoria in the simultaneous game at Hobart was their first first-class victory since 1853/54 ... when NSW beat Queensland by 2 runs in December 1903, the junior state needed 293 to win in the fourth innings, but collapsed from 274-5 and 287-6 to be all out for 290.

Two of first-class cricket's nine innings of 199* were played in double-header matches – by Frank Druce (left) in 1895, and by Reg Hawson in 1912/13. For Hawson, this remained the highest score of his career.

Once Queensland entered the Sheffield Shield in 1926/27, there could be no question of the other states continuing to arrange fixtures with them which coincided with matches against their other Shield rivals. Hence there have been no more double-headers involving Queensland as a junior state from that season on: they were no longer a junior state when they made their last-ever appearance in a double-header, in January 1957. Tasmania's position was a little different. Having played Victoria 75 times between

1850/51 and the last Victorian double-header in 1956/57, their fixtures against their mainland neighbours became much less frequent: they met Victoria twice in each of 1959/60 and 1961/62, and then again only in 1969/70 and 1976/77 (once in each season). But none of these games was played anywhere near a holiday date, and so further double-heading was avoided. The next season, 1977/78, saw Tasmania's long-awaited entry into the Sheffield Shield, so as with Queensland from 1926/27, the prospect of further double-headers involving Tasmania finally ended from that date. And with all the established cricketing states now playing in the Shield competition, none could any longer be treated as a junior, and so the days of double-heading in Australia had finally come to an end.

Australians on tour
These 43 domestic double-headers are not the only ones involving Australian teams.

Between 1883/84 and 1896/97, five Australian 'state' sides (strictly, colonial sides) made brief tours to New Zealand, each playing between four and seven first-class matches. None of the touring sides was fully representative of the strength of their state.

This was particularly the case for the three New South Wales sides that toured in 1888/89, 1893/94 and 1895/96. Of the 31 different players in these three NSW teams, no fewer than 18 had not played first-class cricket before going on tour, and only three of the other 13 had played more than three first-class matches before crossing the Tasman (and even those three had played a mere 7, 8 and 18 matches respectively). As many as 19 of the 31 never played for NSW in a Sheffield Shield match, or in equivalent matches before the Shield was first contested in 1892/93. Ten of the 31 made their *only* first-class appearances on these tours, and a further seven played no other first-class cricket after their tours were over.

Despite the weakness of the NSW tourists, and the fact that the first two tours were not officially sanctioned by the NSWCA, the first-class status of their tour matches against New Zealand provincial sides has never been seriously called into question. And weak though they may have been by Australian standards, the touring sides were good enough to win 11, and lose only two, of the 17 first-class matches played over the three tours.

While these sides were playing under the name 'New South Wales' in New Zealand, back home the state's First XI was busy with inter-state/Sheffield Shield matches. Sure enough, there were a number of occasions when both NSW sides were playing at the same time, to give us chronologically our first international double-headers:

Season	Play dates	Fixture	Venue	Result
1889/90	25-27-28-29-30 Jan	**NSW** v Victoria	Sydney	W
	30-31 Jan	Auckland v **NSW**	Auckland	D
1889/90	14-15-(17)-18 Feb	**NSW** v S Australia	Sydney	W
	14-15 Feb	Otago v **NSW**	Dunedin	W

1893/94	26-(27)-29-30 Jan	**NSW** v Victoria	Sydney	W
	27-29 Jan	Wellington v **NSW**	Wellington	D
1895/96	13-14-16-17 Dec	**NSW** v Queensland	Sydney	W
	14-16-17-18 Dec	Canterbury v **NSW**	Christchurch	W
1895/96	26-27 Dec	Wellington v **NSW**	Wellington	W
	26-27-28-30-31 Dec	Victoria v **NSW**	Melbourne	W
	30-31 Dec-1 Jan	New Zealand v **NSW**	Christchurch	L

The pair of games in 1893/94 coincided with one of the double-headers listed in the previous table, but in that 'domestic' instance the side doubling up was Victoria, not NSW. So although this occurrence is memorable as being the only time that two Australian sides double-headed simultaneously, we must wait a little longer for our first 'triple-header'.

Memorabilia from these games:
- R.W. (Bob) McLeod took 3 wickets in 4 balls for Victoria in NSW's second innings at Sydney in January 1890; his brother C.E. (Charlie) McLeod achieved the same feat in NSW's first innings in the double-heading match at the same venue four years later.

- Arthur Coningham (151) made the first-ever first-class century for Queensland in the match at Sydney in mid-December 1895.

- Syd Callaway took 14-65 and 15-175 against Wellington and New Zealand respectively in the two matches over Christmas and New Year 1895/96, with 17 of his 29 victims dismissed 'bowled' and a further three 'caught and bowled'.

Of the other two 'state' tours to New Zealand, neither that by Tasmania in 1883/84 nor that by Queensland in 1896/97 involved any double-heading with those states' sides in Australia. Tasmania played no matches in Australia in 1883/84, and the Queensland side thirteen years later was back home long before the state's only domestic match of the 'home' season, which took place in mid-April 1897.

For our only other set of double-headers by Australians on tour we must move forward half a century and more, though we're staying in New Zealand, at least in part. Although New Zealand played their first Test match in 1930, Australia met them only once at this level until the 1970s. This was in a hugely one-sided match in March 1946 that was only recognised as a Test match a couple of years later. While declining to send their full Test team to New Zealand for the next 28 years, Australia kept the flame alive by sending a second-string side to visit their neighbours on five occasions between 1945/46 and the eventual resumption of Test relations in 1973/74. Three of these five tours - in 1949/50, 1966/67 and 1969/70 - coincided with Test tours to South Africa by Australia's bona fide Test squad, and on each occasion both touring sides were frequently in action on the same days.

The convention is that these touring sides were known as 'Australians' other than in Test matches, when they became 'Australia'. It is a moot point whether the sides that played representative matches against the full strength of New Zealand should also be called 'Australia', since these were not official Test matches; but this is the style that has been adopted by the ACS and CricketArchive, and I shall follow it here.

Following these conventions, the double-headers that occurred over the course of these three 'twin tours' were these:

Season	Play dates	Fixture	Venue	Result
1949/50	17-18-20 Feb	Griqualand West v **Australians**	Kimberley	D
	17-18-20 Feb	Auckland v **Australians**	Auckland	D
1949/50	10-11-13 Mar	W Province v **Australians**	Cape Town	D
	10-11-13 Mar	Otago v **Australians**	Dunedin	W
1966/67	17-(18)-20-21 Feb	South African XI v **Australians**	Pietermaritzburg	D
	17-18-20 Feb	Canterbury v **Australians**	Christchurch	L
1969/70	26-27-28 Feb	Otago v **Australians**	Dunedin	W
	27-28 Feb - 2 Mar	Natal v **Australians**	Durban	D
	2-3-4 Mar	NZ Under-23 XI v **Australians**	Napier	W
1969/70	5-6-7-9-10 Mar	South Africa v **Australians**	Port Elizabeth	L
	6-7-9-10 Mar	New Zealand v **Australia**	Auckland	D
1969/70	17-18-19 Mar	Northern Districts v **Australians**	Hamilton	D
	19-20-21 Mar	Orange Free State v **Australians**	Bloemfontein	W
	21-23-24 Mar	Central Districts v **Australians**	New Plymouth	D

Just a few highlights:

· The match at Christchurch in February 1967 featured John Gleeson's one and only first-class half-century - a score of 59, made from the exalted position (for him) of number nine in the order.

· In the New Zealand Under-23 side's total of 145 in their first innings at Napier in March 1970, the third-highest score off the bat was a mere 6.

· Ian Redpath scored 152 against OFS in March 1970, including a wholly uncharacteristic few minutes when he took 32 runs off a single over (666644) from medium-pacer Neil Rosendorff .

As with the MCC on some of their tours (see page 86), there were also a number of occasions when 'Australia' were playing in one match at the same time as the 'Australians' were playing another in a different continent. These were not true double-headers within our definition, but are worthy of note nonetheless:

· South Africa v Australia (Port Elizabeth, 5th Test) and Canterbury v

Australians (Christchurch) in 1949/50. Simultaneous playing dates were 3 and 4 March 1950.

· South Africa v Australia (Port Elizabeth, 5th Test) in 1966/67 overlapped with the Australians' matches against Auckland at Auckland (simultaneous playing dates 24-25-27 February 1967) and against Central Districts at Palmerston North (28 February).

· South Africa v Australia (Johannesburg, 3rd Test) and Canterbury v Australians (Christchurch) in 1969/70, with simultaneous play on 20-21-23 February 1970.

· And with the boot on the other foot, the only 'Test match' on Australia's tour in New Zealand in 1949/50 was played on exactly the same dates - 17-18-20 March 1950 - as the Australians were playing a South African XI at Johannesburg.

· Similarly, the second 'Test' between New Zealand and Australia at Christchurch in 1969/70 coincided with the Australians' match against Western Province at Cape Town. Simultaneous playing dates were 13 and 14 March 1970; play in both matches was also scheduled for 16 March, but rain prevented any play on this day at Christchurch.

Near misses

Until the 1927/28 season most interstate games in Australia, including those in the Sheffield Shield competition, were timeless: that is, they were played to a finish no matter how long it took. It was only the fact that some of these matches were completed relatively quickly that prevented further additions to the list of domestic double-headers. For example, in 1896/97 a timeless match between Tasmania and Victoria began at Launceston on 20 January 1897 and was completed on 22 January, while on 23 January the NSW v Victoria fixture began at Sydney. Similarly in 1923/24 a timeless match between South Australia and Victoria began at Adelaide on 15 February 1924 and was concluded on 20 February, while on the following day Victoria began a match with Tasmania at Hobart. In both these cases there would have been overlap between Victoria's matches - and hence double-headers - if the earlier-started matches had run into a further day. The near-miss instance in 1896/97, like the three instances noted on page 92, would have featured two 'away' games for Victoria.

In cases such as these, as with the genuine double-headers, the double-heading or potentially double-heading state would have had to select separate squads for the two fixtures. The same was also true on occasion in the 'post-timeless' period, even though no actual or prospective double-heading was in prospect. Thus in 1937/38 and 1949/50, although actual playing dates did not coincide, the programme (and the travelling distances involved) required two separate Victoria squads for a Shield game and a friendly against Tasmania: in the former season, Victoria played Tasmania at Melbourne from 1-3 February 1938 and started a Shield game against South Australia at Adelaide on 4 February, while in the latter season they played Tasmania at Melbourne from 24-26 January 1950 and began a Shield game against NSW at Sydney on 27 January.

Apart from these instances, the closest approach to a further double-header in Australia came during West Indies' inaugural tour in 1930/31. The season's fixture list scheduled Victoria to play Queensland in the Sheffield Shield in Brisbane from 31 January to 4 February 1931, and to play the West Indians at Melbourne on exactly the same dates. The two separate sides were selected, and the game at Melbourne duly went ahead, with what amounted to a Victoria Second XI holding out for a draw against the tourists thanks to an unbroken last wicket partnership of 30 in the fourth innings. Meanwhile the Shield side travelled to Brisbane, only to see their game abandoned without a ball bowled because of rain. So no double-header after all.

Mention should also be made of a near-triple-header recorded by Victoria in 1912/13. At the same time as two Victorian sides were playing their double-header against NSW and Tasmania beginning on 24 January 1913, a Victoria Colts XI was playing NSW Colts at East Melbourne (also 24-25-27-28 January). As Ray Webster has pointed out[82], the Victoria Colts XI included five players who represented Victoria in first-class matches in the same season, and four others who played first-class cricket in the following season. Although there could be no question of the Colts side's being given first-class status, it is arguable that it was a side of 'first-class standard', whatever that means; the outcome of a fixture between it and the Victoria side that played against Tasmania at the same time would surely not have been a foregone conclusion. Here are the three Victorian elevens that played on those dates – you may judge their relative merits for yourself:

v NSW (Sheffield Shield)	*v Tasmania (first-class friendly)*	*Colts v NSW Colts (not f-c)*
E.V.Carroll (24/13)	H.O.Smith (3/2)	A.E.Brown (0/6)
H.H.G.Bracher (0/7)	R.G.Johnstone (2/1)	M.D.Hotchin (1/3)
F.A.Baring (4/26)	C.Dwyer (2/1)	H.C.A.Sandford (1/9)
J.A.Seitz (18/2)	C.Kiernan (1/9)	**R.L.Park** (1/35)
W.W.Armstrong (197/72)	W.I.Sewart (5/8)	C.B.Willis (0/72)
J.Ryder (4/173)	P.A.Shea (0/3)	A.E.Liddicut (3/59)
E.L.Carroll (1/3)	E.L.Spencer (1/1)	J.M.Fitzpatrick (0/1)
T.J.Matthews (53/14)	R.L.Braid (3/2)	F.G.Moule (0/0)
W.Carkeek (82/13)	R.H.Bailey (0/1)	F.L.Lugton (0/5)
H.W.Hart (6/4)	J.L.McNaughton (2/6)	W.Geddes (0/0)
W.H.Cannon (1/6)	J.R.H.Woodford (14/1)	W.R.F.Macrow (5/0)
Lost by 8 wickets	Lost by 54 runs	Drawn. Their opponents included **T.J.E.Andrews** and **Arthur Mailey**

Bold type indicates once or future Test cricketers. The figures given for each player are the number of first-class matches played before, and excluding, the match on 24 January 1913, and the number of first-class matches played after, and including, the match on that date.

A final batch of Australian near-misses is considered in Chapter 10.

---

82   Ray Webster: *First-class cricket in Australia Vol. 1 1850/51-1941/42* (1991), page 499.

6: South Africa -
Welcome to the triple-header

The history of double-headers in South Africa has three phases, the third of which provides our first examples of triple-headers. Let's take them one at a time.

Phase 1 - Before 1959/60

Domestic cricket in South Africa in this period was focussed on the inter-provincial Currie Cup. This began as a challenge competition in 1889/90, and grew in stages to a league competition which from 1946/47 onwards featured nine teams. These nine participants, in chronological order of their first matches in the competition, were Transvaal, Griqualand West (initially known as Kimberley), Western Province, Natal, Eastern Province, Border, Orange Free State, Rhodesia, and North Eastern Transvaal.

The Currie Cup was not contested in seasons when South Africa was hosting a major tour from overseas, and in some other seasons too. Among the latter was 1928/29, when the more important business was to put together the strongest possible side to tour England in 1929. To this end, a series of 12 trial matches was arranged between mid-December 1928 and early January 1929, all played on turf wickets in either Durban or Cape Town. At the time only the first seven teams just named contested the Currie Cup, but one of these – Transvaal – was by a distance the strongest, having won or shared the Currie Cup the last four times it had been contested. For the purposes of the trial matches they were judged strong enough to field two separate teams. The trials thus involved eight teams, with four based at each venue. In effect the events at Durban and at Cape Town – in which each team played one match against each of the other teams in its group – constituted two separate tournaments, although the matches themselves were friendlies, with only pride (and individual players' performances) at stake.

The two Transvaal sides were not in fact or in name distinguished as being the province's First and Second XIs. Both were known simply as 'Transvaal', and the Transvaal union split their strength more or less evenly between them, with nine past or future Test cricketers playing in the team at Durban, and six at Cape Town. The Durban and Cape Town squads were mutually exclusive, except that H.G. 'Nummy' Deane played in two of his side's three matches at Durban before moving west to play in two more at Cape Town. As Transvaal captain, and eventual captain of the 1929 tour party, it was perhaps only to be expected that he would take the opportunity to play with, or against, as many candidate-tourists as possible.

The tournament at Durban ran from 15 to 26 December, and that at Cape Town from 24 December to 3 January. They thus overlapped over the immediate Christmas period – and sure enough, the two Transvaal sides were both involved in matches during this overlap period, with the side at Durban meeting Border while that at Cape Town took on Eastern Province. Thus we have our first South African double-header.

The two matches were scheduled for three days' play each, that at Durban on 22-24-26 December, and that at Cape Town on 24-26-27 December. The two games followed remarkably similar courses: in both of them Transvaal ran up similar big scores on the first day (445 v Border at the Old Fort ground at Durban, of which the first J.P.Duminy made 168*, and 452-6d against Eastern Province at the Wally Wilson Oval at Cape Town, with centuries from Fred Susskind and Charles McKay), and then bowled out their opponents twice on the second day of play. In each case this second day was 26 December, as rain had prevented any play at Durban on Christmas Eve; this was therefore the only date on which both matches were in progress simultaneously. At Durban on this day, Border were dismissed for 115 and 109; Duminy starred this time with the ball in the first innings with 6-40, but only managed 1-21 in the second, in which the most successful bowler was Bruce Mitchell with 5-33. Meanwhile at Cape Town Eastern Province made 110 and 121, with Frank Walsh and Quintin McMillan each taking nine wickets in the match (Walsh 6-35 and 3-42, McMillan 3-24 and 6-48).

If you now do the maths you'll discover the most remarkable of all the similarities between the two matches: the results were exactly the same, with Transvaal winning both of them by precisely an innings and 221 runs. You couldn't have made it up.

The decision to allow two Transvaal sides to play in the trial matches was seen to be justified by the results at each tournament. As all the trial games were friendlies there were no overall winners and losers at the two venues, but if there had been, and if points had been awarded on the same basis as was then current in the Currie Cup, the Transvaal sides would have won both tournaments. Perhaps surprisingly, only eight of the 16 players then selected for the England tour came from Transvaal, though these included both the captain and vice-captain (Deane and Herbie Taylor) and the two

Jacobus Petrus Duminy – no close relation to the Jean-Paul Duminy of more recent vintage – included three Tests in his 13-match first-class career in the 1920s. The 168* that he scored in a double-header match in December 1928 was his only first-class century, and the 6-40 that he took in the same match his only first-class 'five-for'.

wicket-keepers (Jock Cameron and Edward van der Merwe). Despite his success against Border, Duminy was not included in the tour party, as his performances in the other games at Durban were nothing to write home about, though he later briefly joined the tour in England when a number of the tourists were ill or injured. Less surprisingly, Transvaal players dominated the Test XIs in England, with as many as six appearing in both the first and fifth Tests, and five in each of the other three matches. Their continuing strength was shown when they again won the Currie Cup in the following season of 1929/30.

Now we move forward 17 years from the first South African double-header. In 1945/46 cricket was still emerging from wartime privations. There had been no Currie Cup cricket since 1937/38, and although it proved possible to draw up a substantial programme of first-class matches for the first season after the war – 18 games were arranged in all – it was decided that the Currie Cup should not be contested.

Like the 1919 season in England, this was something of an experimental season, as the provincial sides sought to establish which of their pre-war players were still available and in form for the first-class game, and to identify the new talent that might stand them in good stead for the future. Thus Transvaal, for example, played eight matches but used as many as 35 different players, 14 of whom were making their first-class debuts. Their season began with two overlapping two-day (but nevertheless first-class[83]) fixtures in mid-December 1945, against NE Transvaal at Johannesburg and against Natal at Durban. And thus we have the third first-class double-header in South African cricket history (fear not – we'll come to the second one in a moment; but it was a bit different from the other two).

As 17 years earlier, both games in 1945/46 ended in exactly the same result – but this time rather less excitingly so, as both were drawn. At Durban, a Transvaal side containing nine past or future Test cricketers was bowled out for 158, whereupon the opposing Natal side (with 'only' seven Test players) collapsed from 67-0 to 96 all out, with Norman Gordon and Xenophon Balaskas each taking five wickets; Natal's opener Dennis Dyer carried his bat for 49*. Transvaal's second innings reached 193, but in the 54 eight-ball overs remaining Natal did not chase the 256 needed for victory, and ended on 160-3 (Billy Wade 74*, the only half-century of the match). Meanwhile at Johannesburg a definitely second-string Transvaal side, with four first-class debutants, managed a small first-innings lead over their northern rivals (231 to 223), and then declared at 160-4 leaving NE Transvaal to get 169 for victory in what turned out to be 24 eight-ball overs. The challenge was declined as NE Transvaal fell to 14-3 and 45-4 before holding out for a draw on 127-6. Top score of the game was 83 by Richard Martin in NE Transvaal's first innings, while no bowler took a five-for for either side.

The remaining double-header in Phase 1 – chronologically the second of the three in this Phase – once again features Transvaal as the double-heading side, but unlike in the two other instances the matches concerned

---

83   These games pre-dated the ruling in 1947 that to qualify for first-class status matches had to be scheduled for a minimum of three days' play.

were most definitely not mere friendlies. For in 1936/37 Transvaal actually played two overlapping matches both of which were in the Currie Cup competition – the first of all the instances examined in this book so far in which both the games in a double-header were matches in the premier national domestic competition. Sadly I do not have details of the circumstances which brought about this unlikely turn of events. Suffice it to say that on New Year's Day 1937 Transvaal – then, as usual, the Currie Cup holders – began a fixture with Western Province at Cape Town, on the last scheduled day of which they also began a match against Border at Johannesburg.

As Currie Cup points were at stake in both matches, Transvaal divided their resources more or less evenly between them. Of the XI who had played in Transvaal's previous fixture, six (including three once or future Test players) played in the fixture at Cape Town, and four (also including three Test cricketers) stayed at home for the match against Border.[84] The balance of the Transvaal XI against Border included three other Test cricketers, while the balance against Western Province had 'only' two.

Although Transvaal had the better of both games, they could only force a victory in one of them. Against Western Province they secured a big first-innings lead (455 to 217), thanks mainly to an innings of 161 by Syd Curnow. Declaring at 186-7 in their second innings, they left their opponents to make 425 to win, but after losing two early wickets Western Province reached a creditable 331-4 by the time stumps were finally drawn. The game ended with an unbroken stand of 213 for WP's fifth wicket between Bryan Wallace (81*) and Henry van der Spuy (121*), both of whom made their career-best scores in the process. To this day, this remains Western Province's record fifth-wicket stand against Transvaal or its successor side, Gauteng.

The Transvaal side at Johannesburg was more successful, despite conceding a first-innings lead. Border were dismissed for 294 in their first innings, which must have been a disappointment for them as they had been 215-1 and 251-2. They then bowled Transvaal out for 274, but when they went in again Border continued their first-innings collapse, and were reduced to 46-8[85] before a ninth-wicket stand of 105 between Sinclair Hubbard (51*) and Clive White (60) helped them to a final total of 160. Transvaal needed 181 for victory, and reached their target for the loss of only two wickets.

On recent results, Transvaal might have expected to have won both these games, and so dividing their resources between the two matches might not have been thought too much of a risk. Although they ended the 1936/37 season in, for them, a lowly second place in the Currie Cup table, their failure to force victory at Cape Town did not affect this placing: the two

---

84   One of the XI from the previous game, Test bowler Chud Langton, played in
      neither match.

85   Across their two innings, Border at one stage lost 15 wickets while adding only
      73 runs, and 16 wickets for 89 runs, moving from 251-2 to 294 all out in their
      first innings, and then faltering their way to 30-7, and 468, in their second.
      No one bowler dominated in the first-innings collapse, but that in the second
      innings was chiefly the work of 'the man from the ministry' Lennox Brown,
      who took six of the first seven wickets to fall.

extra points they would have obtained if they had beaten Western Province would not have been enough to allow them to pip Natal for the top spot.

So over the course of 17 years, Transvaal played three double-headers. At the time these were the only such instances in South African first-class cricket. No single player appeared in matches in all three double-headers, though several appeared in two of them. The closest approach to playing in all three was by Syd Curnow, who played in the Border fixture in 1928/29 and the Western Province game in 1936/37, and who also appeared for Transvaal in 1945/46 but, sadly, not in either of the early-season double-header games. Bother.

For consistency with previous chapters, the first three South African double-headers may be tabulated as follows:

Season	Play dates	Fixture	Venue	Result
1928/29	22-(24)-26 December	**Transvaal** v Border	Durban	W
	24-26 December	**Transvaal** v E Province	Cape Town	W
1936/37	1-2-4 January	W Province v **Transvaal**	Cape Town	D
	4-5-6 January	**Transvaal** v Border	Johannesburg	W
1945/46	16-17 December	**Transvaal** v NE Transvaal	Johannesburg	D
	17-18 December	Natal v **Transvaal**	Durban	D

Because I have defined double-headers as meaning only matches in which two teams played simultaneously while bearing the same name or representing the same cricketing entity, matches between or involving sides from within the same political-administrative area do not automatically constitute double-headers. In practice, in the period covered by Phase 1 the administrative area of Cape Province contained four fully-fledged first-class sides – Eastern and Western Provinces, Border and Griqualand West; and after the separation (for cricketing purposes alone) of NE Transvaal from the rest of that province in 1937, the administrative province of Transvaal included two distinct first-class sides. But simultaneous matches involving two or more of the sides from within Cape Province, or involving the two sides in Transvaal province, do not meet our definition of double-headers, and are therefore not detailed here.

During researches for this chapter I have come across just one 'near-miss' in South Africa that falls chronologically into Phase 1. According to the fixture list for 1957/58 printed in the *South African Cricket Annual 1957*, a side named Transvaal B were due to play North Eastern Transvaal at The Wanderers on the same dates (1, 2, 4 November 1957) as Transvaal were playing Natal in a friendly at Kingsmead (there were no Currie Cup matches this season because of the Australian Test tour; note also that at this time, no 'B' sides had yet entered the Currie Cup, so for such a side to have played a first-class match would have been a new departure). The annual's fixture list distinguished first-class from non-first-class matches, and the Wanderers game is not identified there as 'not first class' – from which I infer that, at the time that list was printed, the Transvaal B match was regarded as a first-class fixture. But in the event it was denied that status, and so although both matches were duly played, they did not constitute a first-class double-header.

Phase 2 - From 1959/60 to 1998/99

In 1951/52 the Currie Cup competition was split into two Sections, A and B, with one-up one-down promotion and relegation between them. The top four sides from the previous year's competition - Transvaal (champions again, though only for the first time since the war), Natal, Western Province and Eastern Province - made up Section A, with Border, Griqualand West, North Eastern Transvaal, Orange Free State and Rhodesia in Section B. Unlikely as it may seem, Transvaal finished bottom of Section A in that first season, and were relegated to Section B for 1952/53, to be replaced in the top division by OFS.

Transvaal were in Section B for only one season, and things were back to normal for them when in 1958/59 they won Section A with 15 points from six matches. But the other three teams in the Section, Natal, Rhodesia and Western Province, all ended on 13 points. So how to decide which team should be relegated? And at the same time, how best to ensure suitable competition for the players who might be contenders for places in the 1960 touring team to England? To address these questions, the South African Cricket Association [SACA] did some out-of-the-box thinking, as described in *Wisden* in 1960:

"With the 1960 tour of England in view, and the triple tie for second (and last) place in the top section, [SACA] decided to promote Border [winners for the first time of Section B] and to add another team, possibly Transvaal 'B', to the lower section".[86]

In other words, with no clear relegation candidate from Section A, it was decided to enlarge that Section to five teams by giving Border their duly-earned promotion, and to keep the B Section up to five teams by bringing a completely new, tenth, side into the competition. But who should that tenth side be?

As the teams already competing in the Currie Cup already provided full geographical coverage of the Union of South Africa, as well as neighbouring Southern Rhodesia, there was no obvious geographically-based side available to make up the numbers in Section B. Cricket was not sufficiently well established in South Africa's other Commonwealth neighbours, nor in its 'trust territory' of South West Africa, for these to be serious contenders for the tenth place. In the end, as *Wisden* had foreshadowed, the lot fell on a second team from Transvaal - though quite why Transvaal is not clear. Maybe it was simply because they had won the Currie Cup in the previous season; or maybe it was because of their historical strength (by this time Transvaal had won the Currie Cup outright on 13 occasions, four more than any other side); or maybe it was their contemporary strength as measured by the number of Test players in their ranks, in which they comfortably surpassed any of their rivals.

Whatever the reasons may have been, for the 1959/60 season a second Transvaal side was admitted to Section B of the Currie Cup competition,

---

86   *Wisden* 1960, page 879.

to bring the number of teams in each Section up to five. The admission of this second Transvaal side to the Currie Cup is described in Brian Bassano's history of the period as "a decision which was to become as controversial as the splitting of the provinces into two sections in 1951/52".[87] Unfortunately he gave no detail of this controversy elsewhere in his book (and neither does he of the apparent 1951/52 controversy), so we are left to wonder exactly what form it took.[88]

Thus in 1959/60 and subsequent seasons, two Transvaal sides, known as Transvaal and Transvaal B, competed in the Currie Cup. As long as they remained in separate Sections, the two sides would be spared the potential embarrassment of meeting each other; to make certain that this never happened, the competition rules were amended to preclude the relegation of the 'A' side[89], or the promotion of the B side. Thus when Transvaal B won the B Section in 1962/63, 1969/70, 1974/75, 1976/77 and 1984/85 they were not promoted, and when the senior side finished bottom of Section A in 1974/75 and 1975/76 they were not relegated. The same provisions applied when other B teams joined the competition in later years.

In particular, these rules meant that in 1974/75 when Transvaal finished bottom of Section A in the same season as Transvaal B won Section B, the sides did not swap places, even though the normal one-up one-down promotion and relegation rules would have allowed them to do so. There was, of course, opportunity for those who had done well in the B team in 1974/75 to become the core of the Section A side for 1975/76 - and vice versa - but this did not happen in practice.

It is also worth mentioning that Transvaal B did actually finish ahead of Transvaal in the Currie Cup in one season. This was in 1960/61, when for one year only the Currie Cup reverted to a single league. But this was not an 'all play all' league, and so the two Transvaal sides still did not meet. Transvaal B, with a weaker fixture list than the senior team, ended the season in fourth place out of ten, two places above their own first eleven.

Right from the start of the new arrangements in 1959/60, Transvaal's 'A' and B squads were not mutually exclusive. The two sides were simply the province's first and second elevens, as selected match-by-match. Thus in that first season, eight of the 16 players who represented Transvaal in Section A also played, in the same season, for Transvaal B in Section B. But players generally had to make their way through the ranks before reaching Section A: all of the eight cricketers who made their first-class debuts when representing Transvaal in 1959/60 (who, incidentally, included Ali Bacher and Eddie Barlow) made their first appearances in the B team.

During this first season of 1959/60, there were six occasions when Transvaal and Transvaal B played first-class matches simultaneously.

87 Brian Bassano: *South African Cricket Volume 4 1947-1960*, Cricket Connections International, 1996.

88 Surprisingly, the contemporary *South African Cricket Annuals* make no comment on the background to, or even the fact of, the admission of a second Transvaal side to the Currie Cup.

89 The senior side was officially known simply as Transvaal and the junior side as Transvaal B, and this same naming practice was later adopted by the other unions as other B sides were admitted to first-class competitions. Where necessary to distinguish the sides, I refer to the senior side as the 'A' side.

The first of these double-headers was on 20 November 1959, when the senior side began a Section A match against Border at Johannesburg , at the same time as the B side was making its first first-class appearance, against Griqualand West at Kimberley. The occasion was a double success for Transvaal, who recorded innings victories in both matches.

As a means of increasing the amount and competitiveness of first-class cricket in South Africa, other provincial 'B' sides were successively admitted to the Currie Cup competition, or its successors, as follows:

	First and last seasons as a first-class side	Total number of first-class matches played
Transvaal B (a)	1959/60 – 1996/97	195
Natal B (b)	1965/66 – 1998/99	178
Western Province B	1975/76 – 1998/99	131
Eastern Province B	1977/78 – 1998/99	113
Rhodesia B (c)	1977/78 – 1979/80	14
Northern Transvaal B (d)	1981/82 – 1998/99	88
Orange Free State B (e)	1989/90 – 1995/96	30
Boland B	1993/94 – 1995/96	15
Border B	1993/94 – 1995/96	15
Griqualand West B	1998/99	6

(a)   Played as Transvaal B throughout – never as 'Gauteng B'

(b)   Played as KwaZulu-Natal B in 1998/99

(c)   Played as Zimbabwe-Rhodesia B in 1979/80. Rhodesian sides withdrew from South African domestic competitions following Zimbabwe's independence in 1980.

(d)   Played as Northerns B in 1997/98 and 1998/99. Never played as 'North Eastern Transvaal B'.

(e)   Played as Free State B in 1995/96

The figure for the number of matches played includes occasional games outside the Currie Cup and its successors.

The double-headers played by these teams over these periods are too numerous to detail separately. In practice, the majority of the B sides' matches coincided or overlapped with matches played by the senior provincial sides – hardly surprising, given that the domestic fixture lists were generally drawn up with games in Sections A and B being played simultaneously. In total, the numbers of such double-headers by each side were as follows; the figures for Transvaal and Natal each include two instances where one of the matches concerned was not a Currie Cup match.

Transvaal	133	Orange Free State	15
Natal	117	Boland	12
Western Province	73	Border	11
Eastern Province	69	Griqualand West	6
Northern Transvaal	50	Rhodesia	5

In the great majority of cases, these double-headers involved one provincial side playing at home while the other played away. There were however seven occasions when both provincial XIs played at home simultaneously – as Surrey had done in 1909, but as has not happened in any of the other double-headers noted previously in this book. Here are brief details of these instances:

Season	Play dates	Fixture	Venue	Result
1979/80	15-16-17 Mar	**Zimbabwe-Rhodesia** v E Province	Bulawayo	L
	15-16-17 Mar	**Zimbabwe-Rhodesia B** v Transvaal B	Salisbury	D
1982/83	12-13-15 Nov	**Northern Transvaal** v Natal	Pretoria	D
	12-13-15 Nov	**N Transvaal B** v Orange Free State	Benoni	L
1982/83	2-3-4 Dec	**Eastern Province B** v Boland	Port Elizabeth	D
	4-5-6 Dec	**Eastern Province** v Northern Transvaal	Port Elizabeth	D
1983/84	3-4-5 Nov	**Northern Transvaal B** v E Province B	Pietersburg	D
	4-5-7 Nov	**Northern Transvaal** v Transvaal	Pretoria	D
1986/87	1-2-3 Jan	**Natal** v Northern Transvaal	Durban	D
	1-2-3 Jan	**Natal B** v Boland	Pietermaritzburg	D
1994/95	11-12-13-14 Nov	**Western Province** v Orange Free State	Cape Town	L
	11-12-13 Nov	**W Province B** v Western Transvaal	Cape Town	W
1997/98	20-21-22-23 Feb	**Northerns** v Eastern Province	Centurion	L
	20-21-22 Feb	**Northerns B** v Easterns	Pretoria	W

There were thus three instances when a provincial side was playing two matches simultaneously in the same city or conurbation. In December 1982 Eastern Province's game against Northern Transvaal was played at the main ground in Port Elizabeth (St George's Park) while their B team was playing at the ground of the University of Port Elizabeth; in November 1994 Western Province played OFS at Kingsmead while their B team was playing Western Transvaal at the ground of Tigers CC in the Cape Town suburb of Parow; and in February 1998 Northerns were playing in the Pretoria suburb of Centurion while their B team were occupied at the L.C.de Villiers Oval near the city centre. But we shouldn't get too excited about the proximity of these matches. The two grounds in Port Elizabeth are over 7.5km apart (straight-line distance), the two in Pretoria some 14km apart, and the two in Cape Town over 15km apart, so if you were an avid spectator you couldn't just pop out of one game and into the other. (For comparison, the straight-line distance between Lord's and The Oval in London is about 6.5km.)

The propriety of granting first-class status to 'B' XIs was under challenge throughout the 1990s. After much to-ing and fro-ing over the years on the subject, their first-class status - and the scope for double-headers involving provincial A and B XIs - was finally withdrawn after the 1998/99 season.

Since 2004/05 there have been two separate domestic first-class competitions in South Africa. The more senior - the direct descendant of the Currie Cup - is currently (2012/13) known as the Sunfoil Series, and features 'franchise' sides that take the best players from the various combinations of provinces that they represent. The junior competition is the CSA Three-Day Provincial Competition, which currently features 14 sides broadly aligned with the old provincial unions, but including separate sides for KwaZulu-Natal and KwaZulu-Natal Inland, along with a new side representing South Western Districts (the area immediately east of Cape Town), and a new 'overseas' side from Namibia. For the record, the KwaZulu-Natal and KwaZulu-Natal Inland sides represent separate cricket unions (with their headquarters at Durban and Pietermaritzburg respectively), and so simultaneous matches by these two sides do not meet this book's definition of a double-header as one involving two teams with the same name or representing the same geographical or cricketing entity.

With their best players creamed off for the Sunfoil Series, the provincial sides in the CSA Three-Day Competition may be regarded as something akin to 'second elevens'. But unless there is a radical restructuring of domestic cricket in the future, it seems as though the days of genuine double-headers in South Africa is now finally over. Its end had come in February 1999 with these instances:

Season	Play dates	Fixture	Venue	Winners
1998/99	25-26-27-28 Feb	Boland v **Griqualand West**	Paarl	Drawn
	26-27-28 Feb	North West v **Griqualand West B**	Fochville	NW
	25-26-27-28 Feb	Eastern Province v **KwaZulu Natal**	Port Elizabeth	EP
	25-26-27 Feb	**KwaZulu Natal B** v Western Province B	Durban	WP B
	25-26-27-28 Feb	**Western Province** v Border	Cape Town	Drawn

Phase 3 - 1971/72 to 1990/91
Phase 3 overlaps chronologically with Phase 2, for reasons which will become apparent.

This being South Africa, the teams that we have looked at so far, at least until the early 1990s, were 'whites only'. But alongside the matches played under the auspices of SACA, the governing body of whites-only cricket in apartheid days, competitive inter-provincial matches were also being played by non-racial teams, under the auspices of the South African Cricket Board of Control (SACBOC; from 1977/78, the South African Cricket Board, or SACB). In 1971/72 these matches began to be played over three days, which meant that, for the first time, they met one at least of the criteria for being classified as 'first-class'. SACB inter-provincial games continued until 1990/91, the last season before unified cricket finally came to the country under the newly-formed United Cricket Board of South Africa (UCBSA).

Towards the end of the 1990s the UCBSA ruled retrospectively that the three-day inter-provincial games played under the auspices of SACBOC/ SACB between 1971/72 and 1990/91, together with a small number of representative games from the same period, should be ranked as first-class. Following assembly of the scores of the matches concerned by devoted statisticians in South Africa, that ruling has since been accepted by the majority of statisticians worldwide, including by the Association of Cricket Statisticians and Historians in 2006.[90]

This ruling brings into play the possibility of further double-headers, based on the part of the definition given in the Introduction to this book which refers to teams representing the same geographical area - even though, in the iniquitous circumstances then applying in South Africa, the two provincial sides assuredly were not representing the same cricketing entities, as the SACA and SACBOC/SACB provincial administrations were entirely separate from each other.

Only four SACBOC/SACB provincial sides – those representing Transvaal, Natal, and Eastern and Western Provinces – played in the three-day, first-class competitions, and so it was only these four sides who could have participated in matches simultaneously with their SACA namesakes.

This actually happened on a large number of occasions. There were in total 162 occasions when a SACBOC/SACB team was playing a match at the same time as *either* the SACA 'A' or 'B' team from the same province, and a further 79 occasions when a provincial SACBOC/SACB side was playing a first-class match at the same time as *both* the SACA A and B teams were playing. These 79 instances finally give us our first triple-headers, with three teams in the field at the same time each representing the same geographical area and bearing the same name (apart from the 'B' suffix for the SACA unions' second elevens). These matches break down between the provinces as follows:

	Double-headers	Triple-headers	Seasons of first and last triple-headers
Transvaal	39	25	1971/72 – 1988/89
Natal	36	26	1971/72 – 1990/91
Western Province	41	14	1975/76 – 1989/90
Eastern Province	46	14	1977/78 – 1990/91

The triple-headers most commonly took place over the Christmas and New Year holiday periods. Western Province actually recorded as many as four triple-headers in the 1980/81 season , in instances starting on Boxing Day 1980, 30 December 1980 or 1 January 1981, 15 or 16 January 1981, and 19 or 21 February 1981.

Again, the number of double- and triple-header instances identified during

---

90   See the *ACS International Yearbook* for 2007, page 361.

this Phase is too great for them all to be listed separately here. But for the record, the first and last triple-headers ever played in South Africa were as follows; italics indicate SACBOC/SACB fixtures. In the 'first' instances, both Transvaal and Natal recorded triple-headers on the same dates.

Season	Play dates	Fixture	Venue	Winners
First				
1971/72	26-27-28 Dec	**Transvaal** v W Province	Johannesburg	Drawn
	26-27-28 Dec	*E Province* v **Natal**	Port Elizabeth	Natal
	27-28-29 Dec	**Transvaal** v **Natal**	Johannesburg	Tvl
	27-28-29 Dec	**Natal B** v **Transvaal B**	Ladysmith	Tvl B
Last				
1990/91	5-6-7 Jan	Natal v **E Province**	Pietermaritzburg	Drawn
	5-6-7 Jan	OFS B v **E Province B**	Bloemfontein	Drawn
	5-6-7 Jan	*E Province* v *Natal*	Port Elizabeth	EP

We will encounter triple-headers again shortly.

7: Pakistan -
Last home of the double-header

The complicated background

When the state of Pakistan was created in 1947, three of the teams that had been competing in India's Ranji Trophy found themselves in the new country – Sind (based at Karachi), Northern India (based at Lahore), and North West Frontier Province (NWFP, based at Peshawar). Lahore and Karachi were already established as the main cricketing centres in the new country, the former having already hosted 38 first-class matches and the latter 21. Only four cities in All-India had hosted more first-class matches by this date than Lahore (Bombay 168, Madras 62, Poona 55 and Calcutta 43), while Karachi was ninth on the list (behind also Delhi, Secunderabad and Patiala).

The pattern continued in the early days of cricket in Pakistan, where 16 of the first 19 first-class matches, to 1952/53 inclusive, were played at either Karachi or Lahore.[91] When the first domestic first-class competition, the Quaid-e-Azam Trophy (hereafter 'QeA'), was set up in 1953/54, seven teams participated, comprising five geographically based sides (Punjab [successors to Northern India], Sind, NWFP, and two more recently-established sides from Karachi and Bahawalpur) and two from national organisations (Railways and Combined Services). East Pakistan and Baluchistan also entered the QeA in 1953/54 but withdrew before the competition started; they both participated in the tournament's second season, in 1954/55.

Bahawalpur and Karachi were the first two winners of the QeA, but these first two seasons showed up the widely divergent strengths of the competing sides. To address this, for the next holding of the competition in 1956/57, Karachi and Punjab were each allowed to enter three teams. The continuing focus of the game on Karachi and Lahore was thus still in evidence. The three teams from Punjab were distinguished by letters (they were known as Punjab, Punjab A and Punjab B), but those from Karachi adopted the later-customary pattern of distinguishing the sides by using colour-names, being known as Karachi Blues, Karachi Greens and Karachi Whites. Although cricket in East Pakistan (now Bangladesh) was weak by comparison with that in the west, East Pakistan also entered two teams in the QeA for 1956/57, and they followed the Karachi pattern by being named Greens and Whites.

So began an arrangement that has continued in Pakistan to the present day, whereby the stronger geographically-based sides – and on occasion, the stronger departmental (company) sides too – have been allowed to enter more than one team in particular domestic competitions. The provinces and departments [from here on I use the word 'organisations' to cover provinces and departments collectively] that have taken advantage of this arrangement are as follows.

---

91   The others were one each at Bahawalpur, Rawalpindi and Sialkot

Karachi	1956/57 to date	Rawalpindi	1964/65 to 1995/96
East Pakistan	1956/57 to 1970/71	Railways	1965/66 to 1971/72
Punjab	1956/57 to 1977/78	Hyderabad	1969/70
Sind	1957/58 to 1976/77	PIA	1969/70 to 1973/74
Lahore	1961/62 to date	National Bank	1975/76

The dates given are of the organisations' first and most recent 'doublings', but – as the next table will show – in many cases the periods of doubling (or in some cases tripling) by particular organisations have been far from continuous between these dates. A full list of the doubling and tripling first-class organisations, by season and by competition, is as follows:

Doubling and tripling first-class organisations in Pakistan

Season	Tournament	
1956/57	QeA	**East Pakistan** Greens/Whites; **Karachi** Blues/Greens/Whites; **Punjab**/A/B*
1957/58	QeA	**East Pakistan** A/B; **Karachi** A/B/C; **Punjab**/A/B**; **Sind** A/B
1961/62	QeA	**Karachi** Blues/Greens/Whites; **Lahore** A/B
1962/63	QeA	**Karachi** A/B; **Lahore** A/B
1963/64	QeA	**Karachi** Blues/Whites; **Lahore** Greens/Whites
1964/65	QeA	**Karachi** Blues/Whites; **Lahore** Greens/Reds; **Rawalpindi** Greens/Yellows
1965/66	Ayub	**Karachi** Blues/Whites; **Lahore** Greens/Reds; **Railways** Greens/Reds
1967/68	Ayub	**East Pakistan** Greens/Whites; **Karachi** Blues/Whites; **Lahore** Greens/Reds; **Railways** Greens/Reds
1969/70	QeA	**Hyderabad** Blues/Whites; **Karachi** Blues/Whites; **Lahore** A/B
	Ayub	**Karachi** Blues/Greens/Whites; **Lahore** A/B; **PIA** A/B; **Rawalpindi** Blues/Greens
1970/71	QeA	**Karachi** Blues/Whites; **PIA** A/B; **Railways** A/B
	BCCP	**East Pakistan** Greens/Whites; **Karachi** Blues/Greens/Whites; **Lahore** Blues/Greens/Whites; **PIA** A/B; **Rawalpindi** Blues/Greens
1971/72	BCCP	**Karachi** Blues/Greens/Whites; **Lahore** A/B; **PIA** A/B; **Railways** A/B
1972/73	Patron's	**Karachi** Blues/Greens/Whites; **Lahore** A/B
1973/74	Patron's	**Karachi** Blues/Whites; **Lahore** A/B; **PIA** A/B
	Punjab	**Lahore** Blues/Greens/Reds
1974/75	QeA	**Punjab** A/B; **Sind** A/B
	Patron's	**Karachi** Blues/Whites; **Lahore** A/B
	Punjab	**Lahore** A/B/C
1975/76	QeA	**Punjab** A/B; **Sind** A/B
	Bhutto	**Karachi** Blues/Whites
	Patron's	**Karachi** Blues/Whites; **Lahore** A/B; **National Bank** A/B
	Pirzada	**Karachi** Blues/Whites
	Punjab	**Lahore** A/B/C

1976/77	QeA	**Punjab** A/B; **Sind** A/B
	Bhutto	**Karachi** Blues/Whites
	Patron's	**Karachi** Blues/Whites; **Lahore** A/B
1977/78	QeA	**Punjab** Greens/Whites †
	Patron's	**Karachi** A/B; **Lahore** A/B; **PIA** A/B
1978/79	Patron's	**Karachi** A/B; **Lahore City** A/B
1983/84	Patron's	**Karachi** Blues/Greens/Whites; **Lahore City** Blues/Greens/Whites
1984/85	Patron's	**Karachi** Blues/Whites; **Lahore City** Blues/Whites
1985/86	Patron's	**Karachi** Blues/Whites; **Lahore City** Blues/Whites
1989/90	Patron's	**Karachi** Blues/Whites
1990/91	QeA	**Karachi** Blues/Whites
1991/92	QeA	**Karachi** Blues/Whites
1993/94‡	QeA	**Karachi** Blues/Whites
1994/95	QeA	**Karachi** Blues/Whites; **Rawalpindi** A/B
1995/96	QeA	**Karachi** Blues/Whites; **Rawalpindi** A/B
1996/97	QeA	**Karachi** Blues/Whites
1997/98	QeA	**Karachi** Blues/Whites
1998/99	QeA	**Karachi** Blues/Whites
1999/00	QeA	**Karachi** Blues/Whites
2000/01	QeA	**Karachi** Blues/Whites; **Lahore** Blues/Whites
2001/02	QeA	**Karachi** Blues/Whites; **Lahore** Blues/Whites
2002/03	QeA	**Karachi** Blues/Whites; **Lahore** Blues/Whites
2004/05	QeA	**Karachi** Blues/Whites; **Lahore** Blues/Whites
2005/06	QeA	**Karachi** Harbour/Urban; **Lahore** Ravi/Shalimar
2006/07	QeA	**Karachi** Harbour/Urban; **Lahore** Ravi/Shalimar
2007/08	QeA	**Karachi** Blues/Whites; **Lahore** Ravi/Shalimar
2008/09	QeA	**Karachi** Blues/Whites; **Lahore** Ravi/Shalimar
2009/10	QeA	**Karachi** Blues/Whites; **Lahore** Ravi/Shalimar
2010/11	QeA	**Karachi** Blues/Whites; **Lahore** Ravi/Shalimar
2011/12	QeA	**Karachi** Blues/Whites; **Lahore** Ravi/Shalimar
2012/13	QeA	**Karachi** Blues/Whites; **Lahore** Ravi/Shalimar

*   *Three teams participated, known as Punjab, Punjab A and Punjab B*

†   *Two teams from Sind (A and B) also entered, but Sind B withdrew from their only scheduled match.*

‡   *There was no doubling in 1992/93, as Karachi Blues had been relegated to the non-first-class second grade of the QeA competition.*

Key to tournaments:

Ayub   *President Ayub Trophy Tournament. First held 1960/61*
BCCP   *Successor (1970/71 to 1971/72) to the Ayub Trophy*
Bhutto   *Sikandar Ali Bhutto Cup (1972/73 to 1976/77)*
Patron's   *BCCP Patron's Trophy, successor to BCCP Trophy from 1972/73.*
Pirzada   *Pirzada Abdul Sattar Tournament (1974/75 to 1975/76)*
Punjab   *Punjab Tournament (1973/74 to 1975/76)*
QeA   *Quaid-e-Azam Trophy: The principal domestic competition, first held in 1953/54. Only the top tier of this competition - known as Grade I, and sometimes split into two divisions - is first-class. The Grade II winners are usually promoted to Grade I - and hence to first-class status - for the following season.*

This listing only shows instances in which two teams from the same organisation took part in the same competition in the same year. There have also been occasions where two teams from an organisation played in one competition in a particular year, but combined to enter a single team in a different competition in the same year - e.g. Karachi entered a single side in the Ayub Trophy in seasons from 1961/62 to 1964/65, when multiple Karachi teams were playing in the QeA. There have also been occasions when only one 'colour' side participated in a particular competition in some years - e.g. Karachi Blues, but no other Karachi side, played in the Patron's Trophy in 1986/87 and 1987/88.

The listing also shows that since the late 1970s only the two traditional centres of Karachi and Lahore – the latter known for a while as Lahore City, to distinguish it from a separate side representing the parts of the Lahore administrative division outside the city, which was known as Lahore Division[92] – have been allowed to enter more than one team in particular competitions on a regular basis, though an exception was, apparently reluctantly, made in the mid-1990s to allow two teams from Rawalpindi to play in the first-class section of the QeA.[93]

Since 1983/84 there have been no instances of an organisation being allowed to enter more than two teams in any competition. That this was a rule rather than just a convention was shown when Karachi Greens won the non-first-class Grade II of the QeA at the end of the 1995/96 season, which would normally have entitled them to promotion to Grade I, but they were denied promotion partly because of a proposed restructuring of the QeA competition for the following season, but also because Karachi already had two sides (Whites and Blues) in the top division.[94]

Finally, the listing shows the preponderant use of colour-names to distinguish one side from another. However, this pattern was broken in 2005/06 when both Karachi and Lahore chose to distinguish their sides by the use of geographical names[95], though Karachi reverted to the colour pattern two seasons later.

As far as it is possible to tell from an analysis of their players, there was no direct correspondence between the Karachi Urban and Harbour sides and the earlier, or subsequent, Blues and Whites, although there was rather more correspondence between the Lahore 'old' and 'new' sides. Thus of those who played for Karachi Blues in 2004/05, four played for

---

92   'Lahore Division' were a separate side - sometimes first-class, sometimes not, depending on the outcomes of promotions and relegations - between 1978/79 and 1998/99, after which the administrative units known as Divisions were abolished. During this period the Lahore Division team was run by a separate Cricket Association from that running the Lahore City sides, and so simultaneous matches by a Lahore City side and a Lahore Division side did not constitute double-headers within the meaning used in this book.

93   The promotion for 1994/95 of Rawalpindi B, Grade II winners in 1993/94, was initially refused after a ruling that only Karachi and Lahore could field more than one team at the top level. This decision was later reversed, in time for Rawalpindi B to participate in full in the 1994/95 QeA. No comparable situation involving 'second teams' from outside Karachi or Lahore has arisen since. (See *Wisden* 1995 p. 1248, and 1996 pp. 1253-4.)

94   *Wisden* 1997, page 1225.

95   Ravi and Shalimar are two of the 'towns' that make up the administrative division of Lahore.

Karachi Harbour in 2005/06, and five played for Karachi Urban; and of those who played for Karachi Whites in 2004/05, six played for Karachi Harbour in 2005/06, and six for Karachi Urban. At the other end of the Karachi 'interregnum', in 2007/08, Karachi Urban played one final match at the start of the season, in the annual challenge match between the winners of the QeA and the winners of India's Ranji Trophy. Of the 11 'Urban' players in this match, two went on to play for Karachi Blues in the 2007/08 QeA, and one for Karachi Whites. The remaining eight all played for departmental sides.

In Lahore there was rather more correspondence between Blues-Ravi and Whites-Shalimar: nine of the 2004/05 'Blues' squad turned out for Ravi in 2005/06, as against only three turning out for Shalimar; while ten of the 2004/05 'Whites' squad played for Shalimar in 2005/06, again with only three turning out for rivals Ravi.

Although this pattern of doubling in domestic competitions in Pakistan may seem like a duplication of the pattern in South Africa from 1959/60, there were two major differences.

The first is that the Pakistani sides – those with colour names, at least – were not actually or implicitly their organisations' First and Second (and Third) Elevens. Leading Pakistan statistician Abid Ali Kazi has confirmed to me[96] that players were and are allocated to one 'colour' squad or another at the start of the season, with a view to distributing player strength evenly. However, while this may be true nowadays, it does not always seem to have been the case – for example, in almost all seasons where an organisation was represented by sides labelled 'A' and 'B' (and sometimes 'C'), the 'A' side ended the season with the best record, which suggests that player-selections were merit-based and designed to identify First and Second (and Third) XIs. The only exception to this pattern came when Karachi C reached the QeA final in 1957/58, ahead of the Karachi A and B teams.

Thus each side has its own separate player-squad, and there can be no switching by a player within one season from one side to another – unlike in South Africa, where players regularly turned out for both the provincial 'A' and B elevens in the same season. However, there was no reason why a player should not move between, say, the Whites and the Blues between seasons, and this happened frequently. As examples chosen at random, Test player Wallis Mathias played in the QeA for Karachi Blues in 1956/57, moved to the Whites in 1961/62, went back to the Blues again in 1964/65, and returned once more to the Whites in 1969/70; while more recently Hasan Raza (the youngest-ever Test cricketer, allegedly) played for Karachi Blues in 1996/97, for the Whites between 1997/98 and 2001/02, and for the Blues again in 2004/05, since which date his domestic cricket has mostly been for Habib Bank.

These examples give some credence to the impression that, at least in the early days in Karachi, the Whites were regarded as the senior side, with the Blues as next best, and the Greens as a team of promising young players. Thus in 1956/57 Karachi Whites included in their sides regular

---

96   In a private e-mail dated 13 October 2008.

Test players Hanif and Wazir Mohammad, Alimuddin, Waqar Hasan and Mahmood Hussain, while the Blues' biggest names were the rather less distinguished Test duo of Maqsood Ahmed and Ikram Elahi. In later years, future Test cricketers Liaqat Ali and Saleem Jaffar were among those gaining their first first-class experience with the Karachi Greens. But as the 1956/57 example illustrates, not *all* the best players went into the Whites squad; so even then, there appears to have been some attempt to mix and match the players, but maybe with some aim of producing a Whites side which was first among equals.

This contention works less well for Lahore, where if anything the Blues were generally stronger than the Whites. And frankly I have no way of assessing the relative merits of the colour sides from other provinces or departments – Rawalpindi Greens against Rawalpindi Yellows in 1964/65 for example, or Railways Greens against Railways Reds in the following season. But barring any firm evidence to the contrary, I am happy to go along with Abid Ali Kazi's statement that the squads, in recent times at least, have been selected in the hope of producing roughly evenly-matched sides. We'll look shortly at how this has worked out in practice.

The second difference from the arrangement in South Africa is that in Pakistan there has never been any absolute restriction on two sides from the same organisation meeting each other in a first-class match. True, in some tournaments played in whole or in part on a knock-out basis, or played in mini-groups before the group winners came together for a concluding series of knock-out games[97], sides from the same organisation were often deliberately kept apart in the earlier stages; but if their results required them to play each other in a knock-out game, then that is what happened. In total there have been 40 instances of such 'internal' first-class matches in Pakistan to the end of the 2012/13 season.

Double-heading

With so many instances of organisations doubling in domestic competitions, occasions when two or more sides from the same organisation were playing simultaneous first-class matches were inevitable, and frequent. The first Pakistani double-header began on 28 December 1956, when Karachi Greens and Karachi Whites opposed each other at the Karachi Parsi Institute Ground. The first instance not involving an 'internal' match came a week later on 4 January 1957, when Karachi Blues met Punjab A at Lahore at the same time as Karachi Whites were playing Sind at Hyderabad. Since then, to the end of the 2012/13 season there have been over 360 further instances, as summarised in the following table. The left-hand column includes all the organisations which have, at one time or another, had two teams in the same competition, even though – as the table reveals – not all of them have been involved in double-headers:

	'Internal' matches	Other double-headers	Total	Seasons of first and last/most recent
East Pakistan	2	0	2	1956/57 – 1957/58
Hyderabad	0	0	0	--

---

97   As was the case with some of the more ephemeral first-class competitions and even, for some years until the late 1980s, with the QeA.

Karachi	26	182	208	1956/57 – 2012/13
Lahore	7	109	116	1973/74 – 2012/13
National Bank	0	0	0	--
PIA	0	5	5	1969/70 – 1977/78
Punjab	2	6	8	1956/57 – 1977/78
Railways	0	4	4	1965/66 – 1971/72
Rawalpindi	2	17	19	1964/65 – 1995/96
Sind	1	2	3	1957/58 – 1976/77
TOTALS	**40**	**325**	**365**	

Lahore and Karachi continue to play double-headers up to and including the 2012/13 season. This leaves Pakistan as the only country where, under present arrangements for first-class cricket, there remains scope for further double-headers to take place – at least on a regular basis.

I do not have space to give full details of all the 360-plus instances of Pakistani double-headers here. Instead, I note in the following sections some of the more interesting matters arising.

(i) Internal matches

Here, summarised, are the results of matches between teams from the same organisation. In cases where a team has won on first innings and thus progressed to the next round of a particular competition, I have counted this as a win for the team concerned. Drawn matches in other circumstances are listed as such.

East Pakistan Two matches: Greens beat Whites; A beat B

Karachi 26 matches in all. In matches between Blues and Whites, Whites currently lead by 12 victories to 8. In other matches, Whites lead Greens 2-0, Blues drew their only match with Greens, A beat B in their only meeting, A drew with C in their only meeting, and Urban beat Harbour in their only meeting.

Lahore Seven matches in all. Blues lead Whites 2-0, with one draw; in other matches, Greens beat Blues, A beat B, and Shalimar have beaten Ravi in their only two meetings to date.

Punjab Two matches, both between Punjab and Punjab B, and both drawn

Rawalpindi A have beaten B in their two meetings

Sind A drew with B in their only meeting.

Some memorable games:

· In 1962/63 Karachi A and Karachi B met in the final of the QeA, when Karachi A won by an innings and 163 runs. The A side included nine past or future Test players, the B side only four (and those decidedly less distinguished). Brothers Antao and Marshall D'Souza played on opposite sides, for the As and Bs respectively.

· The following season, Karachi Blues defeated Karachi Whites in the QeA final, by a margin of just 18 runs. This time the Blues had five Test cricketers against the Whites' eight. There was some correspondence between, on the one hand, the former A team and the Whites, and on the other, the former B team and the Blues. But this did not prevent a very different outcome from the teams' meeting of the previous year.

· The first two meetings of teams from Lahore were also in finals – namely, the finals of the Punjab Tournaments of 1973/74 and 1974/75. In the former, Lahore Greens beat Lahore Blues by an innings and 91 runs, although the Blues had more past or future Test players in their ranks (three against two). In 1974/75 the rivals had become Lahore A and Lahore B, with the A team winning on first innings; the only three Test players in the game all represented Lahore A.

· In the Patron's Trophy in 1989/90, and again in the QeA competition in 1995/96, Karachi Whites met Karachi Blues on two occasions in the same competition – once in the league matches, and again in the final; and in both finals, the result of the earlier league meeting was reversed. In 1989/90 the Blues had beaten the Whites by six wickets in the league, but the Whites won the final by one wicket, with their last-wicket pair of Nauman Mushtaq and Fakhruddin Baloch adding 34 runs to see them home. In 1995/96 the boot was on the other foot: the Whites won the league game by five wickets after forcing the Blues to follow on, but in the final the Blues were the victors by 59 runs, despite trailing on first innings by 116.

· The only other time when the same two teams have contested internal matches twice in the same season was in 1993/94, when Karachi Whites beat their Blue rivals both in the league match between them (won by 10 wickets) and in the competition semi-final (won on first innings). The Whites came unstuck in the final, however, in which they were beaten by nine wickets by Lahore City, the only Lahore side in the QeA that season.

· Apart from those already mentioned, the only other innings victories in internal matches have been in 1956/57, when Karachi Whites beat the Blues by an innings and 132 runs – the Whites scored 762 (Hanif Mohammad 228) in their only innings; in 1957/58, when East Pakistan A beat their B side by an innings and 80 runs; and in 2001/02, when Lahore Blues beat the Whites by an innings and 18 runs.

You may draw your own conclusions from the above details about the relative strengths of the different sides from the same organisations. In my view they broadly corroborate Abid Ali Kazi's statement that the 'colour' sides were selected to be roughly equal in quality, whereas sides called 'A' seem consistently to have been superior to Bs and Cs.

A further indication that neither of today's sides in Karachi, and neither of those in Lahore, is regarded as the city's 'first team' is the fact that, especially in recent years, they have shared the principal grounds in the city, rather than one side always having first call on the main ground. Thus between 1996/97 and 2012/13 inclusive, on the 37 occasions when Karachi Blues and Whites have played separate but simultaneous home matches, the Blues have played at the National Stadium (the principal

Test venue in the city) on 18 occasions and the Whites on 16, with three instances where both teams were playing elsewhere. At Lahore there has been a slightly greater imbalance: of the 28 separate but simultaneous home matches played by Ravi and Shalimar since 2005/06, Shalimar have played 15 at the Gaddafi Stadium against only seven by Ravi, with six occasions where neither team used the Test ground. This imbalance largely dates to the earlier part of the period, as Ravi did not play their first match at the premier ground until 2010/11, since when they have played there seven times against Shalimar's four.

(ii) Triple-headers

The presence of three teams from the same organisation in one competition in the same year has created the potential for all three teams to be playing simultaneously on occasions, and this has actually happened six times, as follows – with the triple-heading team being Karachi on each occasion. In the instances in 1957/58 (11 October) and 1983/84 (11/13 October), two of the three matches were against sides from the same province, making these occasions double-headers for the teams from Sind and Lahore City respectively, as well as triple-headers for Karachi.

Season/Tmt	Play dates	Fixture	Venue	Winners
1957/58 QeA	11-12 Oct	**Karachi A** v **Sind B**	Karachi	KA
	11-12 Oct	**Karachi B** v Quetta	Karachi	KB
	11-12-13 Oct	**Karachi C** v **Sind A**	Karachi	KC
1957/58 QeA	25-26- 27 Oct	**Karachi A** v **Karachi C**	Karachi	D
	25-26- 27 Oct	Punjab A v **Karachi B**	Lahore	KB
1969/70 Ayub	20-21 Feb	**Karachi Blues** v Quetta	Karachi	KB
	20-21-22 Feb	Punjab Univ v **Karachi Greens**	Lahore	Punjab U
	20-21-22 Feb	Sargodha v **Karachi Whites**	Sargodha	KW
1970/71 BCCP	19-20 Jan	**Karachi Blues** v Hyderabad	Karachi	KB
	19-20-21 Jan	Bahawalpur v **Karachi Whites**	Bahawalpur	D
	19-20-21 Jan	**Karachi Greens** v Multan	Lahore	KG
1983/84 Patron's	11-12-13 Oct	**Karachi Blues** v **Lahore City Blues**	Karachi	KB
	13-14-15 Oct	Bahawalpur v **Karachi Greens**	Bahawalpur	D
	13-14-15 Oct	**Lahore City Whites** v **Karachi Whites**	Lahore	D
1983/84 Patron's	18-19-20 Oct	Gujranwala v **Karachi Whites**	Gujranwala	KW
	18-19 Oct	**Karachi Blues** v Quetta	Karachi	KB
	18-19-20 Oct	Multan v **Karachi Greens**	Sahiwal	Multan

(iii)   Simultaneous home matches

With so many double-headers in Pakistan – and particularly in Karachi and Lahore – it will come as little surprise to find that there have been numerous occasions when an organisation has played two simultaneous matches at home - or on one occasion three, as noted in the first entry in the preceding table. In fact there have been over 100 such instances, the great majority in the two main centres, but also including three in Rawalpindi. There are too many instances to set out the details here. The first was on 25-27 January 1957, when Karachi Blues played Railways at the Karachi Gymkhana Ground at the same time as the Karachi Greens were playing Sind at the Karachi Parsi Institute Ground. The pattern has continued right up to the 2012/13 season, which featured six such instances, three involving the Karachi teams and three involving those from Lahore.

8: Zimbabwe - Late starters

Senior domestic cricket in Zimbabwe – then part of the colony of Rhodesia – began in 1903/04, with the first competition for the Logan Cup. The cup was initially contested by teams representing Mashonaland, Matabeleland, and Midlands, and these three were later joined by Manicaland and, for a while, a team from Northern Rhodesia. The competition – not yet first-class – was held in most subsequent years, but was almost invariably a two-horse race between the sides from Mashonaland (with players essentially drawn from the city of Salisbury) and Matabeleland (drawing largely from Bulawayo). By 1967/68, the cup had been won outright 23 times by Mashonaland and 22 times by Matabeleland, with only single wins by Midlands in 1951/52 and by Northern Rhodesia in 1964/65 interrupting the two giants' hegemony.

1967/68 marked Matabeleland's last success in the competition for over 25 years, as teams from Mashonaland won every tournament from 1968/69 to 1994/95 inclusive. Such was Mashonaland's dominance over this period that for some seasons the inter-provincial competition was not held, with the cup being awarded instead to the winners of the National League club competition. Even when the Logan Cup became a first-class competition in 1993/94 (following Zimbabwe's admission as a full member of the ICC), the familiar pattern of success for a side from Salisbury – now Harare – continued, for a couple of seasons at least.

But the winners since the late 1960s were not always a side called simply 'Mashonaland'. In 1968/69, and again in 1987/88 and 1988/89, the winners were 'Mashonaland A', while in 1980/81, 1981/82 and 1992/93 they were Mashonaland age-group sides – the Under-25s in the 1980s, and the Under-24s in 1992/93. Such was the dominance of Mashonaland that it was clearly judged to be fairest if its talent were spread over a number of teams. Not that this prevented their sides from winning, but at least it allowed for some closer competition, and a little more uncertainty over the outcome of individual matches.[98]

The same pattern continued into the Logan Cup's first-class period. In 1996/97 and again in 1999/2000 Mashonaland was represented by a single side (and unsurprisingly won the cup both times), but in all other years up to and including 2001/02 it had two or even three teams in the competition, as follows:

1993/94 and 1994/95	Mashonaland, Mashonaland Under-24, and Mashonaland Country Districts
1995/96	Mashonaland, Young Mashonaland, and Mashonaland Country Districts
1997/98-1998/99, and 2000/01-2001/02	Mashonaland and Mashonaland A

I have sought advice from John Ward, expert on all things to do with cricket in Zimbabwe, as to the separateness of these teams. Did they all represent the same cricketing entity, and how rigidly was the separation

---

98   The material regarding the early history of the Logan Cup is derived from an article on the competition on page 67 of *Zimbabwe Cricket Year 1998*.

between them enforced in terms of player quality, age, or geographical origin? Here is the gist of his reply[99]:

> "Mashonaland and Mashonaland A both represented the same entity, the Mashonaland Cricket Association. They were largely, but perhaps not quite, the province's first and second elevens respectively, but Mashonaland A was strengthened by a few (maybe very few) top players like Stuart Carlisle.

> "All the sides [i.e. Mashonaland, Mashonaland A, Mashonaland Country Districts – hereafter MCD – and the age-group Mashonaland sides] were basically under the umbrella of Mashonaland, although there is (or was) an MCD Association – but I am not sure how autonomous it was. MCD teams were basically for players born, raised or living outside Harare. If there was no separate MCD team, then MCD players were eligible to represent other Mashonaland teams. Some MCD players lived in Harare but had links in the past with Districts, thus enabling MCD to claim them as players to help them form a viable team. As well as MCD being able to claim anybody if they could show a genuine Districts connection, there were some players (like the Campbells) who could have been claimed by MCD but played in the main Mashonaland team, and vice versa. I'm not sure how agreement was reached, but I am not aware of any controversies."

Closer investigation of the distinctions between the various Mashonaland teams bear out John Ward's statements about the relative standings of the Mashonaland and Mashonaland A sides. For example, in 1997/98 the 'Mashonaland' squad included eleven cricketers who had already played Test matches for Zimbabwe, while the 'Mashonaland A' squad included none. This balance changed somewhat over the next few years – in 1998/99 the figures were 10-3, in 2000/01 8-5, and in 2001/02 5-6 – but the strongest players (such as Eddo Brandes, Alistair Campbell, Andy Flower, Paul Strang and, when available, Murray Goodwin) were invariably in the 'Mashonaland' squad. Stuart Carlisle was probably the strongest 'regular' in the A side; as John suggests, it is possible he was placed into that squad to give it a little more beef. The biggest-name player who moved between the sides was Grant Flower, who was in the top squad for the first three of the seasons referred to, but moved to the A squad in 2001/02.

The fact that, in 1997/98 at least, the two Mashonaland sides were 'first and second elevens' is confirmed by a reference on page 67 of *Zimbabwe Cricket Year 1998*, where it is stated that "A close competition [for the Logan Cup] is currently impossible to achieve, as in the past two years the Mashonaland first team [sic] has thrashed all opposition out of sight. It would be more competitive were the top Mashonaland players distributed between two evenly-balanced teams, but the Zimbabwe Cricket Union, afraid of pressure from the ICC, is unwilling to do so."

As for the age-group sides, the apparent age-limits were not adhered to rigidly. In 1993/94 the oldest player in the Mashonaland Under-24 squad (wicket-keeper Blessing Ngondo) turned 24 during the season, which seems fair enough. Ngondo and another player born one day later than

---

99   Edited from an e-mail dated 10 September 2009.

him were still playing for the Under-24s the following year, but they were both 'out-dated' by Australian-born Shaun Prescott, who had played two matches for Victoria in 1989/90 and who made his debut for Mashonaland Under-24s in March 1995 when nearer his 29th birthday than his 28th. The renaming of the side as 'Young Mashonaland' for the 1995/96 season was perhaps done to address such inconsistencies, though in fact the oldest player in the side in that year (Grant Flower) was only 25 when the season began. The distinction between 'young' and 'old' also does not seem to have been maintained very rigidly, with the best players going to the 'Mashonaland' side even if their age qualified them for the age-group sides. Thus for example, in that 1995/96 season, five of the players who appeared for 'Mashonaland' were younger than Grant Flower, and as many as seven of the 15 cricketers who turned out for 'Young Mashonaland' were older than the youngest players in the 'Mashonaland' squad.

Finally, on the 'Country Districts' issue, it seems that birthplace alone was very definitely not the key qualification. Of the 17 cricketers who played for MCD in 1993/94, 13 are shown in the 'usual sources' as having been born in Salisbury, two more in Bulawayo, and only two somewhere else in Zimbabwe. In 1994/95 the figures were 12 from Salisbury, 4 from Bulawayo, 1 from South Africa and 4 from elsewhere in Zimbabwe; in 1995/96 those figures became 10, 2, 1 and 6 respectively. What the MCD players' other links - if any - to the more rural parts of Mashonaland Province might have been is not known to the present writer.

As in Pakistan (but not in South Africa), when the province had more than one side in the Logan Cup competition, players were allocated, by whatever means, to a particular squad at the start of the season, and there was no movement of players between different teams during that season. Also as in Pakistan but not South Africa, there was no restriction on sides from the same province playing against each other: indeed, with so few teams taking part, the whole competition would have broken down were such a restriction in place.

During the relevant seasons, matches in the Logan Cup were generally played in a series of 'rounds', with each round beginning on the same day. This has therefore given rise to several double-headers in Zimbabwean domestic cricket: 19 in all, including 12 instances of 'internal' matches between two sides from Mashonaland, and six occasions when two Mashonaland sides were playing simultaneous matches, both of which were at home. Seven of the first eight instances were triple-headers, with three Mashonaland sides playing simultaneously. Here are the details of all 19 instances:

Season	Play dates	Fixture	Venue	Winners
1993/94	14-15-16 Jan*	**Mash CD** v **Mash**	Harare S	D
	14-15-16 Jan	Mat v **Mash U-24**	Bulawayo	Dn
1993/94	11-12-13 Feb*	**Mash** v **Mash U-24**	Harare SC	U-24
	11-12-13 Feb	Mat v **Mash CD**	Bulawayo	Mat

1993/94	4-5-6 Mar	†**Mash** v Mat	Harare SC	D
	4-5-6 Mar*	†**Mash U-24** v **Mash CD**	Harare A	D
1994/95	16-17-18 Sep*	**Mash CD** v **Mash U-24**	Harare S	U-24
	16-17-18 Sep	Mat v **Mash**	Bulawayo	Mash
1994/95	10-11-12 Mar	†**Mash U-24** v Mat	Harare A	U-24
	10-11-12 Mar*	†**Mash** v **Mash CD**	Harare SC	Mash
1994/95	24-25-26 Mar*	**Mash** v **Mash U-24**	Harare SC	Mash
1995/96	15-16-17 Sep	†**Mash** v Mat	Harare SC	Mat
	15-16-17 Sep*	†**Young Mash** v **Mash CD**	Harare A	MCD
1995/96	17-18-19 Nov*	**Mash** v **Young Mash**	Harare SC	Mash
	17-18-19 Nov	Mat v **Mash CD**	Bulawayo	Mat
1995/96	8-9-10 Dec*	**Mash CD** v **Mash**	Harare S	MCD
1997/98	28-29 Aug*	**Mash** v **Mash A**	Harare S	Mash
2000/01	16-(17)-18 Feb	†**Mash** v CFX Academy	Harare SC	Mash
	16-(17)-18 Feb	†**Mash** A v Mat	Harare A	D
2000/01	2-4 Mar*	**Mash** v **Mash A**	Harare SC	Mash
2000/01	9-10-11 Mar	†**Mash** v Manicaland	Harare SC	Mash
	9-10-11 Mar	†**Mash A** v CFX Academy	Harare A	Mash A
2000/01	23-24-25 Mar	**Mash** v Mat	Harare SC	Mash
	23-24-25 Mar	Midlands v **Mash A**	Kwekwe	D
2000/01	30-31/3-1/4	Manicaland v **Mash A**	Mutare	Mash A
	30-31/3-1/4	Midlands v **Mash**	Kwekwe	Mash
2001/02	1-2-3-4 Mar	CFX Academy v **Mash A**	Harare CC	Mash A
	1-2-3-4 Mar	Manicaland v **Mash**	Mutare	Mash
2001/02	22-23-24 Mar	†**Mash** v Midlands	Harare SC	Mash
	22-23-24-25 Mar	†**Mash A** v Manicaland	Harare A	Mash A
2001/02	5-6-7-8 Apr*	**Mash** v **Mash A**	Harare SC	Mash
2001/02	19-20 Apr	CFX Academy v **Mash**	Harare CC	Mash
	19-20-21-22 Apr	Mat v **Mash A**	Bulawayo	D

Internal matches, i.e those between two Mashonaland sides, are indicated by an asterisk against the playing-dates. A dagger against the team-names indicates instances when two Mashonaland teams were playing simultaneous home matches.

Key to grounds in Harare: A – Alexandra Sports Club; CC – Harare Country Club; S – Harare South Country Club; SC – Harare Sports Club (the Test match venue).

The size of the Mashonaland sides' victories in several of these games - they included four innings victories, and another four by over 200 runs

- shows just how great was the margin between that province and many of its rivals, even when Mashonaland's strength was split two or even three ways.

Some memorabilia relating to double-header matches in Zimbabwe:
· There were no double-headers in the Logan Cup 1998/99. Mashonaland and Mashonaland A were due to meet at the Sunrise Sports Club in Harare on 12-13-14 January 1999, but the match was rained off.

· A week later, rain also ruined the prospects for the only scheduled double-header in Zimbabwe that would have involved a game outside the Logan Cup. Mashonaland A were due to play their Cup match against Matabeleland at Bulawayo on 19-20-21 January, while Mashonaland were due to meet England A in a first-class match at the Old Hararians ground in Harare on 20-21-22-23 January. The weather in Bulawayo created no insuperable problems (Matabeleland won their match by 7 wickets), but unfortunately rain in Harare meant that the game there had to be abandoned without a ball bowled.

· In first-class matches between sides from within Mashonaland, the results stand like this: Mashonaland have beaten Mashonaland A three times in three meetings; Mashonaland have played MCD three times, with each side winning one match and one match drawn; Mashonaland have won two, and lost one, of their three matches against Young Mashonaland or the Under-24s; while the three matches between MCD and Young Mashonaland or the Under-24s have ended with one victory for each side, and one match drawn. Mashonaland A have never met either MCD or the Young/Under-24 side.

Some 'achievements' from the double-header matches that *were* played:
· Mashonaland Country Districts' wicket-keeper D.J.R. (Donald) Campbell took seven catches in Matabeleland's first innings in their game at Bulawayo in 1994/95.

· A couple of weeks later, Campbell's brother Alistair – a fine batsman, but with no great reputation as a bowler - returned innings bowling figures of 2.3-2-0-3 for MCD against Mashonaland.

· In the match between Mashonaland and Mashonaland A in April 2002, Grant Flower scored 235* for the 'A' team, but was upstaged by his brother Andy who made 114 and 156* for the senior team – the latter innings taking Mashonaland to a fourth-innings score of 340-3 and a seven-wicket victory.

From 2002/03 to 2004/05, Mashonaland was once again represented in the Logan Cup by just a single side, which not unexpectedly won the cup in all three seasons. There was no competition in 2005/06, and in 2006/07 the five provincial sides[100] were renamed by reference to compass points, becoming Northerns (formerly Mashonaland), Southerns (formerly Masvingo), Easterns (formerly Manicaland), Westerns (formerly Matabeleland) and Centrals (formerly Midlands). This arrangement also

---

100   Manicaland and Midlands had rejoined the competition in 1999/2000, and a side from the province of Masvingo joined in 2006/07 - they would have played in 2005/06 but the competition was put into abeyance for that year.

lasted for three seasons; surprisingly, Northerns won the cup in only one of these seasons, with Easterns the winners in the other two. With only one side from Mashonaland participating in the competition between 2002/03 and 2008/09, there was clearly no scope for any further double-heading during this period.

For 2009/10 five franchise sides replaced the five 'compass-based' sides. Their boundaries were based on the new political subdivisions of the country, which had replaced the former five-province set-up, and thus they did not correspond directly with those of the previous sides. Each of the five franchises is linked to two of the ten cities or administrative provinces into which Zimbabwe is now divided. Three of them relate in whole or in part to provinces which were formerly part of Mashonaland: the Mashonaland Eagles cover the city of Harare and the province of Mashonaland Central; the Mid West Rhinos cover the provinces of Midlands and Mashonaland West; and the Mountaineers cover the provinces of Manicaland and Mashonaland East.[101]   But matches between these franchises are not matches between two sides from the same cricketing or administrative entity, and so – at least, for as long as these franchise arrangements survive unaltered – it seems as though the brief age of the double-header in Zimbabwe is now behind us.

---

101   The other franchises are the Matabeleland Tuskers (Bulawayo and Matabeleland North) and the Southern Rocks (Masvingo and Matabeleland South).

9: More tourists, and more national teams

Late in 2012, there was some dispute as to whether a three-day match played in November at the Dr D.Y.Patil Sports Academy at Navi Mumbai between a side styled 'Mumbai A' and the English tourists could, or should, be accorded first-class status. As another side styled 'Mumbai' was playing a Ranji Trophy match at the same time, this would have been the first-ever first-class double-header in India. However, at the time of writing at least (February 2013), a consensus seems to have been reached among statisticians that the 'A' match should not be regarded as first-class, based on the view that a first-class organisation (Mumbai, in this case) cannot put out two sides simultaneously and have both games regarded as first-class. As the earlier chapters of this book have shown, such a view is not unequivocally supported by precedent; but such seems to be the stance of statisticians in the 2010s.

This instance brought to light a similar instance from 11 years previously, in another part of the world, and I am grateful to Adam Frankowski for making it known. In April 2002, the Indian tourists in the West Indies were scheduled to play against Guyana in Georgetown in a warm-up match before the First Test. But after the fixture-list was announced, Guyana won through to the final of the Busta International Shield, the dates for which overlapped with that of the tour match. Nevertheless, both fixtures went ahead. In the Shield final, Guyana was represented by its full first team, leaving the Indians to be opposed by a second-string side known as the Guyana Board President's XI. All eleven players in this side were from Guyana, and it was, in fact if not in name, the Guyana Second Eleven. Three of the players were making their first-class debuts[102], and at the time of the match none of the others had played more than 35 first-class games. There can be no doubt that the President's XI was in practice representing Guyana, and on that basis this instance meets this book's definition of a double-header because two sides - albeit differently named - were representing the same cricketing entity simultaneously. Thus this instance becomes the West Indies' first, and to date only, first-class double-header.

The Board President's XI match has always been accepted as first-class, though as Adam Frankowski has pointed out, the principal difference between it and the more controversial case involving Mumbai A was no more than that the Guyana Second XI was given a fancy name whereas the Mumbai Second XI wasn't. There is a second difference, in that the Guyana side was not strengthened by international players from elsewhere, as Mumbai A was (the latter included two strong players from outside Mumbai, C.A.Pujara and S.Dhawan, principally to give them match practice): a fact which strengthens the case for awarding the Mumbai game first-class status, if the first-class status of the Guyana game were to be taken as the starting-point.

For consistency with previous chapters, this West Indian instance may be tabulated as follows:

---

102   Two of the three went on to play 11 and 16 first-class matches respectively; the third played no other first-class cricket.

Season	Play dates	Fixture	Venue	Result
2001/02	4-5-6-7 Apr	Jamaica v **Guyana**	Kingston	D
	5-6-7 Apr	**Guyana Board President's XI** v Indians	Georgetown	L

Although the match at Kingston ended as a draw, it should be reported that Guyana won the Shield by virtue of their first-innings lead (354 to 277). Their single-innings score comfortably exceeded the aggregate of the two innings of their second XI (118 and 168) back home in Georgetown.

* * * * *

This seems an appropriate place to mention a category of matches that arguably meets our definition of a double-header, but which stands apart from the instances discussed in the rest of this book.

Since the 1990s, all Test countries have regularly fielded national sides expressly referred to as 'A' elevens, or sometimes as 'B' elevens; or more recently in England's case, as the England Lions. These sides are generally made up of young players regarded as showing promise for possible future Test honours. They sometimes play at home in warm-up matches for touring teams, and sometimes go on tour themselves as a means of gaining experience. Although picked by the national selectors, their squads are chosen using different criteria from those used in selecting the full Test side. There is no intention that they should be seen as fully representative national sides, nor that they are necessarily the national 'second eleven'. Thus when one of these elevens plays a first-class match at the same time as their country's Test team , as has happened surprisingly often, there is no suggestion that the two teams are equal representatives of their country. It is for this reason that I place them apart from the other double-headers considered in these pages.

To mid-November 2012, there have been as many as 86 occasions when a national 'A' or 'B' eleven has played a first-class match that coincided or overlapped with a Test match by the same country: 16 instances each for England A and Sri Lanka A, 15 for West Indies A (and another five for West Indies B), 13 for Pakistan B, 9 for South Africa A, 7 for India A, 3 for New Zealand A and 2 for Australia A. There have been no instances involving Zimbabwe A or Bangladesh A. The first such instance was as early as 1986, when West Indies B played Zimbabwe at Harare on 25-27-29 October (Zimbabwe were not yet a Test-playing nation) at the same time as the West Indies were playing a Test match against Pakistan at Faisalabad. In five of these 86 instances, the Test team and the 'A' team were playing simultaneous home matches: three instances in New Zealand in March 2004 (when Tests against SA at Hamilton, Auckland and Wellington coincided respectively with 'A' side matches against Sri Lanka at Queenstown, Lincoln and Christchurch), and one each in South Africa (v Bangladesh and Sri Lanka A at Potchefstroom and Kimberley respectively in October 2002) and Sri Lanka (v Bangladesh and South Africa A at Colombo and Dambulla respectively in September 2005).

10: A final batch of near misses

The biggest of them all

Of all the near-misses recorded in these pages, none were as significant, or as deliberate, as four that took place in Australia in the 1977/78 season, when Kerry Packer's World Series Cricket teams were playing in Australia at the same time as the official, much weakened, Australian Test team was playing a five-match home series against India. In an effort to attract crowds away from the official games, four of the WSC SuperTests were quite deliberately programmed to coincide with four of the official Test matches - although Mr Packer's rivalry (or business sense) never took him as far as staging his games in the same city as the official Tests. The plan was not a success, as the SuperTest crowds were not all that Mr Packer might have hoped: "WSC's decision to hold their SuperTests on the same dates as the official Test Matches was harmful to their cause, and was another example of their over-confidence".[103]

By all accounts the SuperTests were first-class in everything but name, but the fact remains that they are not, and surely never will be, included in the canon of first-class matches, because they were not sanctioned by the official governing body of cricket in the country where they were played.

That being so, simultaneous fixtures involving Australia in one match, and WSC Australia in the other, cannot be classed as bona fide double-headers. Nevertheless, as noted, during that first season of WSC cricket there were four such coincidences at 'Test level'. Moreover, during each of the four instances, a three-day fixture was also taking place between other teams of Packer's players in the WSC Country Cup, in each case, between sides named WSC Australia and WSC World XI. These were two-innings-per-side matches, but the length of each innings was limited – the first innings to 40 (eight-ball) overs per side, and the second innings to 75 overs; there were also restrictions on the number of overs that individual bowlers could bowl in each innings. Whether, in other circumstances, these games might have qualified as 'first-class' is an open question, but I see no reason why they could not have done.[104]

If these games, as well as the SuperTests, had been regarded as first-class, there would have been four bona fide double-headers in the 1977/78

---

103   Henry Blofeld: *The Packer Affair*, Collins, 1978, page 141.
104   Many first-class competitions around the world have imposed limits on the number of overs bowled in each first innings – for example, the County Championship in 1966 (some matches) and 1974-1980 (all matches), and the 'second tier' first-class competition in South Africa between 2004/05 and 2010/11. However, none that I am aware of have imposed comparable limits on the second innings as well, nor have they limited the number of overs allowed to each bowler. But there is nothing in the official definition of a first-class match which would automatically preclude games played under these conditions from being accorded first-class status.
As for the standard of the games in Australia in 1977/78, in all four cases being considered here the WSC Australia sides in the SuperTests were close to the country's strongest possible XIs, while either nine or ten of the WSC Australia sides in the Country Cup matches were, or would become, (official) Test cricketers; and the opposing West Indies and World XIs were pretty much their full-strength SuperTest sides, except in the fourth match when the World XI's senior players were involved in the SuperTest at Perth. It surely could not be claimed that any of these WSC sides was not up to 'first-class strength'.

season, when two sides called WSC Australia were playing simultaneously (and in one instance their opponents in each case were the WSC World XI). These would become triple-headers if the simultaneous official Tests were also taken into account; they would meet this book's definition because all three of the home sides were representing Australia, even though only one of them was the team of the country's official governing body, and only that one bore the simple name 'Australia'.

Here are the details of these three-way near-misses, with the results given from the perspective of the Australian teams:

Dates of play	Match	Venue	Type	Result
December 1977				
2, 3, 4, 6, 7	Australia v India	Brisbane	Official Test	W
2, 3, 4	WSC Australia v WSC West Indies	Melbourne	WSC SuperTest	L
2, 3, 4	WSC Australia v WSC World XI	Rockhampton	WSC Country Cup	L
16, 17, 18, 20, 21	Australia v India	Perth	Official Test	W
16, 17, 18	WSC Australia v WSC West Indies	Sydney	WSC SuperTest	L
16, 17, 18	WSC Australia v WSC World XI	Canberra	WSC Country Cup	L
30, 31; 2, 3, 4 Jan	Australia v India	Melbourne	Official Test	L
31; 1, 2, 3 Jan	WSC Australia v WSC West Indies	Adelaide	WSC SuperTest	W
31; 1, 2 Jan	WSC Australia v WSC World XI	Geelong	WSC Country Cup	L
January 1978				
28, 29, 30; 1-3 Feb	Australia v India	Adelaide	Official Test	W
27, 28, 29, 30	WSC Australia v WSC World XI	Perth	WSC SuperTest	L
28, 29	WSC Australia v WSC World XI	Hamilton	WSC Country Cup	W

For WSC's second home season, 1978/79, the idea of coinciding the SuperTests with the official Tests (against England) was dropped. The three-day games were also dropped from WSC's minor competitions. Thus there was no potential for any near-miss double- or triple-headers in Australia in 1978/79.

But the position elsewhere was different. The official West Indies Test side toured India and Sri Lanka between December 1978 and February 1979, at the same time as WSC West Indies were involved in 'Packer matches', first in Australia, and later back home in the Caribbean. Although Test and SuperTest dates were not chosen deliberately to coincide or overlap, there were two occasions when they did so, and a third when the official West Indies side was playing a first-class match against Sri Lanka (not yet a Test-playing nation) at the same time as their WSC counterparts were involved in a SuperTest elsewhere. So again, these three instances would have been bona fide double-headers if the WSC matches were rated as first-class. Here are the three instances, with the results this time given from the perspective of the West Indian teams:

Dates of play	Match	Venue	Type	Result
January 1979				
12, 13, 14, 16	India v West Indies	Madras	Official Test	L
12, 13, 14, 15	WSC Australia v WSC West Indies	Melbourne	WSC SuperTest	D
24, 25, 27, 28, 29	India v West Indies	Delhi	Official Test	D
21, 22, 23, 24	WSC Australia v WSC West Indies	Sydney	WSC SuperTest	L
February 1979				
22, 23, 24	Sri Lanka v West Indies	Colombo	First-class match	D
23, 24, 25, 26	WSC West Indies v WSC Australia	Kingston	WSC SuperTest	W

1978/79 was the last season of the Great Packer Rift, and so there could be no further near-misses under his auspices. And with the seemingly-increasing preference around the world for shorter forms of the game ahead of three-, four-, or five-day fixtures, it seems unlikely that any individual entrepreneur, or other unofficial body, will want to stage such 'quasi-first-class' matches in future. So that, surely, is the end of such potential double-headers.

The name's the same

I have defined double-headers as matches involving two sides representing the same entity, or teams with the same name from the same country. Matches involving two sides with the same name, but representing different entities in different countries, therefore fall outside this definition. But for completeness I record here, without further comment, the identically-named teams that have played in different countries over the years.

Team	Country	Seasons as a first-class side	No. of simultaneous matches
Army	England	1912-1939	None
	India	1934/35 only	
Central Zone	India	1951/52 to date	None
	Bangladesh	2012/13	
Combined Services	England	1920 – 1964	None
	Pakistan	1953/54 – 1978/79†	
East Zone (also North Zone and South Zone)	India	1945/46 to date	None
	Bangladesh	2012/13	
Easterns	South Africa	1995/96 to date	None
	Zimbabwe	2006/07 to 2008/09	
Hyderabad	India	1930/31 to date	44 (1962/63 to 2012/13)
	Pakistan	1958/59 to date†	
Northerns	South Africa	1997/98 to date	None
	Zimbabwe	2006/07 to 2008/09	
Punjab	India	1968/69 to date	6 (1974/75 to 2011/12)
	Pakistan	1953/54 - 2011/12†	

Railways	India	1958/59 to date	30 (1958/59 to 1993/94)
	Pakistan	1953/54 – 1995/96†	
Western Province	South Africa	1889/90 to date	None
	Sri Lanka	1990 – 2004/05†	

The symbol † indicates that there have been significant breaks in the team's first-class appearances within the dates stated.

I have only included simultaneous instances in the above table when the two sides concerned have been named identically. Matches involving teams called (for example) East Pakistan Railways, or Hyderabad Blues, or Western Province B etc, have therefore been disregarded. Similarly, I have excluded the longstanding Ranji Trophy side 'Services' from this table; it is only England and Pakistan that have been home to sides called, specifically, 'Combined Services'.

Also under this heading mention should be made of the communal sides in pre-independence India. Teams called 'Europeans' played in the annual Bombay Tournament from 1892/93 until 1945/46, in an annual Presidency match at Madras between 1915/16 and 1947/48, and in a shorter-lived tournament at Lahore between 1922/23 and 1929/30. The Lahore tournament also featured teams called Hindus and Muslims; teams with these names had also been playing in the Bombay Tournament since 1907/08 and 1912/13 respectively. But all these tournaments were held at different times of year, and there was never any overlap between them – which meant that there were never any occasions when two or even three teams of 'Europeans' were playing simultaneously, nor two teams of Hindus or of Muslims.

Billy Gunn in Christine Keeler mode. Principally a batsman, he took the only two 'five-fors' of his first-class career during a double-header match in 1885, and apparently forswore tobacco some time between September 1884 and March 1887.

133

Rather different, but still worth a mention as they involve sides with the same names but in different countries, were two fixtures played between sides styled 'Smokers' and 'Non-Smokers'– one in England in 1884, the other in Australia in 1886/87. These were end-of-tour first-class games in which players from the two countries combined into two elevens for a friendly match. The merits of laying off the weed were clearly shown in the results, with the Non-Smokers winning by nine wickets at Lord's in 1884, and having much the better of a draw at East Melbourne in 1886/87, when they recorded the then-highest innings total in any first-class match (803 all out – and with one man absent). Nottinghamshire's Billy Gunn evidently saw the light between the two matches – he played for the Smokers in the first game, and the Non-Smokers in the second.

And finally ...

To end, something a bit different: a couple of instances where turf wars within a cricket association led to two elevens turning up to represent the same side in one and the same first-class match. There was never really any chance of both sides playing at the same time, but they seem at least peripherally relevant to the subject-matter of this book! There may be other instances, but these are the two that I have noted to date:

On 3 October 1997, two separate Bahawalpur sides, representing different factions from within the Bahawalpur Cricket Association, turned up for their first Quaid-e-Azam Trophy match of the season, against Karachi Blues at the Asghar Ali Stadium in Karachi. The match referee consulted the Pakistan Cricket Board, and chose one of the squads ahead of the other, and the game then went ahead. It ended in a draw, with Bahawalpur winning a close-fought battle for first-innings points.

On 1 December 2005 two rival teams both claiming to represent Himachal Pradesh turned up at Dharamsala for what should have been their second Ranji Trophy match of the season, at home to Tripura. According to *Wisden*, both HP teams attempted to take the field, which conjures up a confrontational image not perhaps entirely in accord with the spirit of cricket. The matter could not be resolved on the day, and the match was, for the time being, abandoned. When the dispute was eventually settled the game was rearranged to be played on Tripura's home ground at Agartala the following month. In this game the now-home side recorded their first victory in 21 years in the Ranji Trophy, beating HP - who included in their side only two of the players who had appeared in their first Ranji Trophy match of the season in November - by the comfortable margin of 130 runs.

Acknowledgements

Double Headers owes its origin to the late George A.Smith of Hove, who made a passing reference to the 1909 instance in an e-mail he sent me in 2005. As well as thanking him for triggering the train of thought that has led to this book - and I'm pleased to say that I was able to thank him personally before his sad death in 2010 - I must also express my special gratitude to the ACS Committee for agreeing to publish the book, and to numerous others who have assisted one way or another in its preparation, in particular:

Keith Booth and Robert Brooke, for invaluable comments on early drafts of Chapters 1 and 2 respectively; Jo Miller and Bill Gordon, successively in charge of the library at The Oval; Andrew Packham of Reigate Priory CC; Abid Ali Kazi and John Ward, for background material relevant to double-heading in Pakistan and Zimbabwe; Chris Overson, for regular assistance from his extensive book collection; Philip Bailey, David Jeater, Neil Leitch, Stephen Musk and Mike Davage, Robby Wilton and Peter Gilbert, and my brother Roy Walmsley for various other invaluable bits and pieces; and librarians and assistants at the Surrey Record Centre (Woking), Birmingham Archives and Heritage Service, the MCC Library at Lord's, and the British Library Newspaper Reading Room at Colindale.

For assistance in locating photographs and in agreeing to their inclusion in the book, I offer particular thanks to Roger Mann, to Bill Gordon and Surrey CCC, to Colin Harris and Josie Lister of the Bodleian Library at Oxford, and to Timothy Caven of Rugby CC and Peter Davis of Moseley CC.

A special word of thanks is due to John Bryant, for his unfailingly constructive comments in his role as editor, and for his general help in knocking the book into shape. Any remaining fused participles are my responsibility alone.

And thanks to Judith as well of course, without whom, nothing.

K.S.W.

Sources and Bibliography

The main sources used in compiling *Double Headers* have been the following:

Books

Philip Bailey, Philip Thorn and Peter Wynne-Thomas, *Who's Who of Cricketers*, Hamlyn, 1993

Philip Bailey, Robert Brooke and others (ed), *First Class Cricket Matches* for seasons 1801 to 1925, ACS Publications, various years

Jack Bannister, *The History of Warwickshire CCC,* Christopher Helm, 1990

Brian Bassano, *South African Cricket Vol. 4 1947-1960*, Cricket Connections International, 1996

British Isles First Class Cricket Matches, ACS Publications, 1976

Robert Brooke and David Goodyear, *A Who's Who of Warwickshire County Cricket Club*, Robert Hale, 1989

John Bryant (ed), *Great Cricket Matches 1772-1800*, ACS Publications, 2010

Complete First-class Match List, 5 volumes, ACS Publications, various dates

Leslie Duckworth, *The story of Warwickshire Cricket*, Stanley Paul, 1974

A Guide to First-class Cricket Matches played in Pakistan, ACS Publications, 1989

Chris Harte, *A History of Australian Cricket*, Andre Deutsch, 1993

Jim Ledbetter and others (ed), *First-class cricket: A Complete Record* for seasons 1926 to 1939, ACS Publications and Breedon Books, various years

David Lemmon, *The History of Surrey CCC*, Christopher Helm, 1986

David Lemmon, *The History of Worcestershire CCC*, Christopher Helm, 1989

H.D.G. Leveson Gower, *Off and On the Field*, Stanley Paul, 1953

William A.Powell, *Cricket Grounds of Surrey*, ACS Publications, 2001

Ray Webster (ed), *First-class Cricket in Australia*, 2 vols, The Author, 1991 and 1997

Philip Whitcombe and Michael Parsons, *The Free Foresters 1856-2006*, Free Foresters CC, 2006

Peter Wynne-Thomas, *The Complete History of Cricket Tours at Home and Abroad*, Hamlyn, 1989

Newspapers
Berrow's Worcester Journal, Birmingham Gazette, Birmingham Mail, Birmingham Post, Evening Despatch [Birmingham], The Field, Manchester Guardian, Surrey Mirror, The Sportsman, The Times, Worcester Daily Times, Worcester Echo, Worcestershire Advertiser & Agricultural Gazette, Worcestershire Chronicle

Annuals and periodicals
ACS International Yearbook, Cricket: A weekly record of the game, The Cricketer, The Cricket Statistician, Playfair Cricket Annual, South African Cricket Annual, Surrey CCC Handbook, Wisden Cricketer's Almanack, Zimbabwe Cricket Year

Websites etc
CricketArchive; Census returns via www.ancestry.com

Unpublished sources
Reigate Priory CC annual reports, various years
Surrey CCC archives

Index

A page number in bold indicates an illustration.